KEY CHRISTIAN

CHRISTIAN BELIEFS

A FAITH FOR LIVING

LION EDUCATIONAL

Text copyright © 1995 Chris Wright
This edition copyright © 1995 Lion
Publishing

The author asserts the moral right
to be identified as the author of this work

Published by
Lion Publishing plc
Sandy Lane West, Oxford, England
ISBN 0 7459 2648 7
Albatross Books Pty Ltd
PO Box 320, Sutherland, NSW 2232, Australia
ISBN 0 7324 1234 X

First edition 1995
10 9 8 7 6 5 4 3 2 1

A catalogue record for this book is available
from the British Library

Printed and bound in Spain.

Acknowledgments

ACT This book has been produced
under the auspices of The
Stapleford Project. The
Stapleford Project is a curriculum
development initiative based at Stapleford
House Education Centre. The Project aims to
produce materials and offer in-service training
to resource the teaching of Christianity in
schools. Stapleford House Education Centre is
the national conference and study centre of the
Association of Christian Teachers. Full details
of courses and publications are available from:
Stapleford House, Wesley Place, Stapleford,
Nottingham NG9 8DP.

Photo Acknowledgments
ACT: 43
Alton Towers: 18
Andes Press Agency: 67, 93, 97 (top), 101, 102
(bottom), 107 (top and bottom left)
Angela Hampton, Family Life Pictures: 22
(bottom left), 42 (top)
Ann & Bury Peerless: 66 (bottom)
Associated Press: 37 (bottom), 56, 57, 59, 88/
89, 103 (bottom)
A. C. Photographics: 31
Barnaby's Picture Library: 32, 68 (bottom)
Chris Wright: 104
Clifford Shirley: 61
Edimedia: 19, 116 (bottom)
Frank Spooner Pictures: 8
GGT Advertising: 103 (top and centre)
Hodder & Stoughton: 71
Hulton Deutsch Collection: 37 (top), 58, 64
(bottom), 75, 114
ICOREC/Circa Photo Library: 123 (bottom)
ITC Entertainment: 44 (top and bottom), 45, 77
James Davis Travel Photography: 83 (top)
Keith Ellis: 109 (bottom)
Larousse: 20 (bottom), 21 (both pictures taken
from RESCUE MISSION PLANET EARTH
by Children of the World published by
Kingfisher Books. Copyright © Peace Child
International)
Last Resort Picture Library: 84 (bottom)
Leeds Postcards: 122
Lion Publishing: 12 (thought bubble), 16 (top),
24 (top), 70 /David Alexander: 24, 48 (left), 65,
95 (bottom), 97 (bottom) /David Townsend:
64 (top) /John Williams: 12 (centre left), 14
(centre left, centre, centre right), 22 (top and
centre right), 34, 76 (right), 84 (centre), 86
(bottom), 94 (bottom left), 107 (centre), 109
(top), 118 (top), 123 (top)
Metropolitan Police Press Office: 86 (centre),
90 (top)
Mirror Syndication International: 30 (bottom),
100, 105
Neil Beer: 7, 26, 102 (top), 107 (bottom centre)
Nick Rous: 68 (top)
Novosti Photo Library: 62
Open Doors: 81
Photofusion: 84 (top)
Photograff: 95
Press Association: 30 (top), 36, 60 (top and
bottom),
Retna Pictures Ltd: 78
Salvation Army: 47
Sarah Medina: 82, 83 (bottom)
Science Photo Library: 6 (bottom left), 14 (top
left, top centre, top right), 17, 20 (top), 29
(centre), 42 (bottom), 92 (top and centre),
117, 119
Sega Europe: 46
Skjold: 54, 72 (bottom), 76 (left), 94 (top and
bottom right), 106, 120
Skyscan Balloon Photography: 72 (top)
Sporting Pictures: 29 (bottom), 79,
108 (top), 111
Susanna Burton: 91

TEAR Fund: 90 (bottom), 115
Tony Stone Images: 16 (bottom), 28,
Topham Picturepoint: 66 (top), 112
Visual Arts Library: 27, 38, 48 (right)
Zefa Pictures: 6 (top right and top left), 10, 11,
12 (bottom right), 40, 80, 85, 86 (top), 108
(centre and bottom), 116 (top), 118 (centre), 121

Text Quotations
Except where otherwise stated, Bible text is
reproduced from the *Good News Bible*,
copyright © American Bible Society,
New York, 1966, 1971 and 4th edition 1976,
published by the Bible Societies/
HarperCollins
Page 11: *Mister God, This is Anna* by Fynn
© HarperCollins Publishers Ltd
Page 15: *The Present, the Ball and the Import*
by W. H. Vanstone taken from *Quarterly
Review of the Community of the Resurrection*
Page 23: *Here I Am!* by Russell Stannard
© Faber & Faber used with permission
Page 39: *The Screwtape Letters* by C. S. Lewis
© HarperCollins Publishers Ltd,
used with permission
Page 49: *John and his Mother's Hands* taken
from *Assemblies for School Children's Church*
by R. H. Lloyd © Chansitor Publications Ltd,
used with permission
Page 58: *Bridge of the River Kwai* by Pierre
Boulle © Fountana, an imprint of
HarperCollins Publishers Ltd, used with
permission
Page 63: *The Lion, the Witch and the
Wardrobe* by C. S. Lewis
© HarperCollins Publishers Ltd,
used with permission
Pages 70/71: *A Crack in the Wall* by Jackie
Pullinger © Hodder and Stoughton
Page 73: David Suchet details based on an
article from *Christian Family* November 1989
Page 79: Kriss Akabusi profile based on
material from *Kriss Akabusi on Track* by
Ted Harrison © Lion Publishing
Page 81: Nikolai Rublenko material based on a
video, *Nikolai*, produced by
Grenville Films Production
Page 89: *Tramp for the Lord* by
Corrie Ten Boom © Hodder and Stoughton
Page 121: Creed taken from
The Gospel According to the Ghetto by
Canaan Banana © WCC

Illustrations Acknowledgments
Lion Publishing: 14, 15, 41, 55, 62/63, 73, 74, 96
(right), 99, 124
Tony De Saulles: 76, 98
Kim Raymond: 33, 50, 87, 88, 101
Shaun Williams: 9, 10, 12, 13, 17, 23, 25, 39, 52,
53, 72, 96 (left), 110, 113, 115

Contents

How to use this book, and what you will find in it

We could call ourselves 'believing people' since all of us believe in something. For example, we all have our ideas about what is right and what is wrong; many people believe in the existence of one God (this is called monotheism), whilst others do not believe in God at all (they are called atheists). This is a book about Christians, about what they believe in and how they try to live their lives. As you read the book you will notice beliefs which Christians share with others, but your attention will also be drawn to those things which make Christianity stand out—those beliefs which are unique to Christians.

In this book you will find a lot of questions which are designed to encourage you to think about what Christians do and believe. There are other questions to help you to think about your own life, about what is important to you. You do not have to be a Christian to learn something useful from this book.

When you read this book you will be encouraged to refer to passages in the Christian holy book, the Bible. Christians use this book to guide them in their beliefs and actions. Your teacher will help you learn how to look up these references. Since different Christians interpret the words of the Bible in different ways it may be useful to start off by looking at the section on the Bible (pages 72–77) so that you are clear at the beginning on how to understand it.

Your World, My World

We all live in the same world, but we don't all see it in the same way. My view of the world is probably different from yours. One reason for this is because we all think different things are important. What I think is important might not be what you think is important. Our beliefs about what is important affect the way we see the world.

How would the following see the view:
someone with a new
    speed boat
a fisherman
a wildlife expert
a poet or artist
you?

Our beliefs and values are like spectacles—they affect the way we see the world.

Before we start looking at how other people see the world, spend a few minutes on a voyage inside your own head.

A different way of looking

Have you ever played a virtual reality computer game? You put a box over your head which is wired up to a computer game. You become part of the game and enter into a different world.

What is really special to you?

Who is really important in your life?

Name one thing which you want to aim for in life.

People with religious belief see life in a different way from people who don't have religious belief. Their beliefs and values affect how they live in the world.

Although these two people are watching the same game they are looking at it in different ways. Can you say why?

Introducing the Christian world view

About a third of the world's population call themselves Christians. We can't understand someone else's world-view unless we look through their 'spectacles'. This book will help you to see the world as a Christian sees it. It will help you to try on the Christian 'spectacles' by introducing you to the beliefs and values of Christians. It is not asking you to believe in these things. This book simply asks you to take some time to understand Christians' points of view.

In order to help you Christianity has been split up into its key beliefs. However, Christians do not split them up in practice. With a jigsaw you need to fit all the bits together before you see what the whole picture is. The same is true with Christianity. The different beliefs are all part of one big jigsaw. As you go through the book you will start to put the pieces together to form the whole picture.

Look at the photo. What things do you think are important to this young Christian—can you tell from the photograph? What else do you think might be important to a Christian?

Brain Engage

1a Draw the outline of a T-shirt. Design your T-shirt on the theme of 'The Things I Value'. You could include, for example, your family. You can use words, picture, cut-outs.

1b In pairs look at each other's T-shirt. What have you learnt about the other person?

2 Think of three people you know quite well.

- Write down their names.
- Under each name say what you think matters—really matters—to them.

3 Collect different newspaper cuttings about one story on one day and mount them on a display with comments to show how people view the same event in different ways.

By yourself try to describe what you think a Christian is.

As a class or group collect your ideas together.

Using the list of words you have collected try completing the sentence: 'A Christian is . . .'

As you read you will also have to think through your own opinions. Different people have come to different conclusions about Christianity. Here are just two:

❝ The Christian world view is just make-believe. They believe these things to make them feel good. ❞

❝ Christianity is certainly true in my life. It makes sense. ❞

Summary

You have looked at what people in the class believe. Now you are going to be looking at what Christians believe.

7

Is Anyone There?

What thoughts and feelings might Catherine Desteville be having as she hangs suspended from the rock face?

A story is told of a man who hung dangerously to a cliff edge, his fingers losing grip as every second ticked by. 'Is anyone there?' he shouted. From deep below he heard a voice reply, 'I am here. Let go and I'll catch you in my arms.' After a few seconds the man shouted again, 'Is anybody else there?'

Although this is only a story it reflects the fact that many people call out in life, often at times of crisis, 'Is anybody there?' Many people believe that God answers them, and their lives change as a result of the reply they get.

BUT... how can we know whether God exists or not?

It has been argued that there are good reasons to say that there is a God. People point to:

- the existence of the world: there must be a Creator

- the detailed design of the world, showing that it was carefully planned

- the way human beings are made and the fact that many believe there is a purpose to life.

Christians believe that in order to know whether God exists people need to put their trust in him. They call this trust 'faith'. They believe that people cannot really know God from the outside: such knowledge is as impossible as the story of the mother who would not allow her son to go into the water until he had learned to swim!

The Bible doesn't ask the question, 'is there anyone there?' Instead, it takes God's existence for granted. It tells the history of people who put their trust in him.

The Bible describes faith in the following way:

> 66 To have faith is to be sure of the things we hope for, to be certain of the things we cannot see. 99
>
> HEBREWS 11:1

An example of a man who had faith in his own abilities is Charles Blondin. He is probably the most daring tightrope walker ever to have lived. On 15 September 1860 he performed one of the most amazing stunts the world has ever seen. Before a large crowd he walked a tightrope 1,100 feet (370m) long stretched 160 feet (53m) above the Niagara Falls. One slip and he would have plunged to his death. On his first walk across he used a balancing rod. Then he returned across the Falls with a wheelbarrow.

But Blondin had not finished. His assistant climbed into the wheelbarrow to make the return journey. The crowd clapped with relief when he reached the other end. 'Do it again!' they shouted. Blondin asked them, 'Do you believe I can do it again?' 'Of course!' they shouted. 'Well, in that case, one of you get in the wheelbarrow and I'll take you across.' They all refused. They would never know whether he could repeat this most famous stunt—they failed to trust him.

Brain Engage

1 Using the stories and pictures on this page explain what you think the word 'faith' means by writing a short story in which people show faith. It could be showing faith in God or showing faith in other people.

2 Think up arguments for and against the existence of God. I have started you off.

Reasons why God exists:	Reasons against the existence of God:
Many people claim that they have experienced God	If there is a God why doesn't he stop the suffering in the world?

3a Read the story of Samuel in 1 Samuel 3. What does this tell us about faith?

3b Do you think anyone can have faith, or only certain types of people?

Extra:

4 Look up the following stories which show people trusting God—having faith in him. Design your own cartoon strip to illustrate one of them: Genesis 12 (Abraham); Luke 1: 26–38 (Mary).

Summary

Christians say there are good reasons for believing in God. They stake their lives on God's existence.

What Is God Like?

When you think of God what idea comes to mind? Here are some pictures which people have of God.

God as magical rescuer

Some people treat God as though he were a magical rescuer. When they are in trouble they shout out to God for help. For the rest of the time they ignore him.

God as policeman in the sky

66 God is up there like some all-seeing policeman. It's a matter of being good. If I'm not he will punish me. 99

God as an old man in the sky

66 He's up there . . . somewhere. He must be old; after all, doesn't it say that he's been around since the beginning of the world? All you have to do is pray to him for things—he's a bit like a cuddly Santa Claus. 99

God as a powerful force

66 You can't see God. It's just a force like the wind. You can only know God exists by the effect that God has—like the wind on the waves. 99

Look at the pictures and images described on this page. Do you know people who think of God in these ways? Which images do you think are helpful? Discuss the points you want to make with a friend.

A personal God

So what do Christians believe God is like?

A loving parent

Jesus taught his disciples to call God 'Abba'—a word used by children when talking to their dad (Luke 11:2, 9–13). This expresses the most important thing Christians believe about God, that God is a person, someone people can relate to, someone who

cares as deeply for everyone as the best parents do for their children. In Isaiah 66:13 God compares himself to a mother. Christians do not believe that God is either male or female.

> **God is a very personal and very close friend of mine. He's like a firm but loving father who accepts me for everything that I am. Like a father he has hopes for me. He also helps me to lead a better life.**
>
> JUSTINE, 21

> **People think that God's like a jerk and all that. And he's not at all, he's really cool.**
>
> TANK, A DRUMMER IN A ROCK BAND

> **When I pray to God I imagine that he's sitting in the armchair in front of me. I try to imagine his eyes understanding and accepting me.**
>
> KERSTIN, 17

> **He is almighty and he's all-powerful. He created the world. He is also a king, so quite often I come into his presence, you know, and say, 'Thank you, Lord, for doing this.'**
>
> MIKE, 15

Summary

Christians believe God is a person with whom they can have a loving relationship.

Mister God, This is Anna

This book is about Anna, a very wise child of five or six. She believes deeply in God, whom she calls 'Mister God'. Fynn is her friend who writes the book. In this extract Anna tries to explain to Fynn how 'Mister God' loves his children—like a father, but much better than any earthly parent:

> 66 *Fynn, you can love better than any people that ever was, and so can I, can't I? But Mister God ain't like us... You see, Fynn, Mister God is different from us because he can finish things and we can't. I can't finish loving you because I shall be dead millions of years before I can finish, but Mister God can finish loving you... There's another way that Mister God is different. Mister God can know things and people from the inside too.* 99

For Anna, Mister God was personal and close to her:

> 66 *I have had for many years a little plaything, a toy... It is simply two circles of heavy copper wire linked together like two links of a chain. On one occasion I was holding it so that the circles stood at right angles to each other. Anna pointed to one of the circles and said, 'I know what that is—that's me. And that's Mister God,' she said, pointing to the other. 'Mister God goes right through my middle and I go right through Mister God's middle.* 99

Brain Engage

1 What is your idea of an ideal parent? Try completing the following sentence with a number of statements covering how you would treat your children, your feelings, your hopes and so on. If I were a parent I would . . .

2 Using the quotes on this page write a paragraph describing how Christians picture God.

3 Look up Luke 12:6–7. What does Jesus say that shows God is interested in every person?

4 What image of God does Anna have? Draw or design a symbol or image that helps to explain the image Anna has of God's relationship with her.

Promises . . . Promises

Friendships and relationships involve promises. When these are broken people feel hurt and at times betrayed.

What are people promising in the two illustrations on the right?

> But you promised me

In pairs discuss the stories which may lie behind the scenes above and the one to the right.

12

The God who makes promises

The Bible contains the long-running story of the relationship between God and his people. The word used to describe this relationship is 'covenant'. A covenant is a promise made between two parties. God made a covenant with the Jewish people—he promised to be their God and in return they promised to keep his commands. God said:

> 66 If you obey and keep my commandments then I will be your God and you will be my people. 99
>
> JEREMIAH 11:4

The Bible tells how God was faithful to his covenant although his people broke their promise over and over again.

God promised the Israelites, through Moses, that they would be his chosen people (Exodus 6:7). He rescued them out of slavery in Egypt. In return they were to keep God's commands. Christians believe God is wholly good. His rules are the standards this good God sets. The Ten Commandments are a summary of what it means to follow God.

The Ten Commandments have greatly influenced the laws of many countries right up to the present day.

They can be divided into two groups. First, the duties to God:

1. Worship no god but God.
2. Do not make images and bow down and worship them.
3. Do not misuse the name of God.
4. Keep the Sabbath as a day for God—a day of rest from work.

Second, the duties to other people:

5. Respect your father and mother.
6. You must not commit murder.
7. You must not commit adultery.
8. You must not steal.
9. You must not give false witness.
10. You must not envy what others have, wanting it for yourself.

Jesus summed up these laws in two commandments:

> 66 "Love the Lord your God with all your heart, with all your soul, with all your mind, and with all your strength." The second most important commandment is this: "Love your neighbour as you love yourself." There is no other commandment more important than these two. 99
>
> MARK 12:30, 31

The average home has the TV on 7 hours and 2 minutes every day. This means that by the time children finish school they will have spent about 12,000 hours in the classroom. They will have spent 20,000 in front of the TV.

The 'images' or 'idols' forbidden in the second commandment can be anything you put at the centre of your life—taking God's rightful place. Is the TV a modern idol? Why do some people think that this idol is dangerous?

Summary

Christians believe that God is wholly good. God makes—and keeps—promises to people and sets standards for them to live by.

Brain Engage

1 Why do you think rules are important?

2 Make a list of ways in which the Ten Commandments are ignored in today's world. You can use a newspaper to help you. Make into a collage.

3 How would the world be different if the Ten Commandments were kept? Give 2 examples.

4 Try to turn the Ten Commandments into positives. For example, 'You must not murder' means 'Let everyone live in safety.'

5 Look up Hosea 11:1–9 and Ezekiel 20:2–24. What do these say about the way God's people broke his promises?

Extra

6 People sometimes disagree about what these commandments mean in practice. Which of the following break the sixth commandment: all, some or none—

abortion, euthanasia, slaughtering animals for food?

Three Into One Does Go!

Study the following three photographs. What have they got in common? What is happening in the photographs?

Three ways of being Kerry. Study the three photographs of Kerry.
How are the photographs the same, and how are they different?

Three ways of being God: Christian belief in the Trinity

How do you describe God? This is a difficult question since it is very hard to describe what you cannot see. It is also very hard to describe something which is like nothing else you know. Christians would say that God is beyond human ability to describe completely. In common with Jews and Muslims they believe in one God. Yet they describe this one God as three distinct persons, because this is how God has revealed himself. They call this idea that God—the Father, Son (Jesus) and Holy Spirit—is somehow 'three-in-one', belief in the *Trinity*.

The Father creates

The Son rescues

The Spirit gives strength

How Christians try to explain this belief

Because the idea of the Trinity is so hard to explain, a number of pictures have been used to help. When someone asked the Irish fifth-century missionary Saint Patrick to explain the Trinity to them he bent down and picked a shamrock.

'This is one plant with one stem,' he said. 'But it has three leaves. The Trinity is a little like this shamrock.'

On his third visit to America Columbus saw what appeared to be three islands. When he got closer he saw that they were not three but one, united at their bases by a strip of low-lying land. He gave the island the Spanish name for Trinity—*Trinidad*. He said that this is what belief in the Trinity means: while we are far from God we see only three persons. When we see God as he is really then we shall find the three persons are one.

The present, the ball and the import

James was brought up in a children's home because his parents had died when he was a baby. On his fifth birthday the Matron decided to buy him a present. He had never had a present before and said, 'That's not a present: I know what that is, it's a ball.' He thought that 'a present' was one thing and 'a ball' was another. He did not realize that the same object could be more than one thing.

In fact the ball was a ball, a present and an import too since it had come from Hong Kong. Later on that week when he heard God described as 'Father, Son and Holy Spirit' he was able to understand that the teacher was not referring to three gods but one and the same God. Each word refers to God in a different way, as God acts in the world.

Brain Engage

1 Can you think of anything which is difficult to explain in words? For example, explain what electricity is to a five-year-old. You can do this using words, pictures or a story.

2 Read the story of Jesus' baptism in Mark 1:10–11. How is God, Father, Son and Holy Spirit, described in this story?

3 What does God as 'Spirit' mean? Can we feel the power and presence of someone even when they are not there in body? Can you think of an example? Describe it in your own words.

4 A woman can be a sister, a mother and a daughter, three-in-one! Are you three-in-one? Give an 'explanation of yourself' as three-in-one. Illustrate your example.

5 Christians find it difficult to explain the belief in the Trinity. Read the story of Columbus and the story of the present, ball and import. Which of these stories best illustrates the Trinity? Explain why.

6 Draw your own logo for the Trinity.

Biblical teaching

The Bible doesn't use the word Trinity to describe God. However, there are passages in the Bible which are the basis for the idea that God is three persons.

Genesis 1—2:4 talks of God creating the world. John 1:1–14 describes Jesus the Son coming to rescue the world from darkness. Acts 2:1–4 describes the coming of the Holy Spirit to give people power. When Jesus sent his disciples out to spread the good news he used the words:

> 66 Go, then, to all peoples everywhere and make them my disciples: baptize them in the name of the Father, the Son, and the Holy Spirit. 99
> MATTHEW 28:19

Summary

Christians believe in one God. They describe God as three persons—the Father, the Son (Jesus) and the Holy Spirit—in one.

15

Who Dunnit?

What takes your breath away? Sometimes an experience or scene can be so beautiful or powerful that it takes our breath away.

 The natural world has always had this effect on people. It has also led them to ask where everything comes from.

What words come to mind when you look at this picture? Write down the words in your book.

Imagine describing the scene to a friend over the telephone. What would you say?

Where does everything come from?

Three students asked other people this question. Here are some of the answers they received:

• Someone designed it

❝ Look at the wings of this dragonfly—it's such a delicate design. There must be a master designer who brought everything into existence. ❞

• It started with a big bang

❝ I believe that it all started off when all the matter in the universe was concentrated into a hot ball. By chance this exploded in a big bang. Matter flew apart, and cooled—forming atoms, then gases and then galaxies. ❞

• It's no accident

❝ Even if it did all start off with a big bang I can't believe it all happened by accident. What made the matter in the first place? It's like the saying—'what came first, the chicken or the egg?' ❞

◦ Brain Engage

1 Draw your own speech bubble. In it give your own answer to the question, 'Where does everything come from?'

2 Look through all the quotes. Which is the most convincing point of view? Why? Which is the least convincing? Why?

16

Look carefully at the picture below. What do you think it is? (*Answer at the bottom of the page.*) This sort of detail is present in all of nature.

A nice line in beauty and detail

'The idea that life was put together by random shuffling is as ridiculous and improbable as the idea that a tornado blowing through a junk yard may assemble a Boeing 747. The aircraft had a creator and so has life.'

PROFESSOR C. WICKRAMASINGHE

Look carefully at your own hand. Try counting the number of lines on it.

Christians believe that the world is not an accident: there is a Creator. They believe that the world itself—in its beauty and detail—points to a Creator who designed it all. This belief is expressed in the first words of the Bible:

> **66** In the beginning, God created the heavens and the earth. **99**
>
> GENESIS 1:1

Everything that exists, including plants, animals and humans, is God's creation.

Richard Cooling is a doctor. He points out the delicate balance in the way the human body works:

66 The thyroid is a small organ in the front of the neck. It produces a hormone. Too much of the hormone and your eyes stick out, you sweat heavily and you rapidly lose weight. Too little of the hormone and your body slows down. I once had a patient who stopped moving altogether!

"The incredible thing is that the difference between having too little and too much is very, very small. The normal amount is equal to one grain of sand in all the blood in the body. The equivalent of two grains would be far too much.

"As a Christian I find it impossible to believe that the human body is the result of chance. Our health depends on delicate balances like that of the hormone. **99**

The human body is just one example: Christians point to many others.

Brain Engage

3 Look again at the photos on this page. If you had to replace them with other photos what would they be? Remember that the point is the wonder and the design in our world.

4a Read the story of creation in Genesis 1—2:4.

4b In groups choose one of the acts ('days') of creation. Make a collage to illustrate this day.

4c As a class produce a frieze for the wall from the biblical account of creation. Use all the collages which the groups have produced.

Extra

5 Some Christians take every word of the story of creation as literally true. Others do not. Find out how different Christians understand this story.

6 Invent a new annual festival called 'Creation Day'. Describe how you would celebrate it. What would it celebrate?

7 Look at the sky at night, at the millions of stars. Write down your feelings as you gaze upwards.

Summary

Christians believe that the world was created and designed by God.

Answer: *The picture shows a detail of a person's eye.*

Is Anyone In Control?

CREATION

THUNDER LOOPER

Have you ever been on a rollercoaster? What does it feel like to whizz down from the top?

What do people think about when they're on a rollercoaster?

Why are some people scared to have a ride on one?

Are you scared of them? If not, why not? If so, why?

People often feel scared if they feel life is out of control, like a young child separated from parents in the supermarket. The reason why parents allow their young children to go on a rollercoaster is that they trust the person who made it. At other times, what matters is having someone near us who we can trust. We feel safe then.

However, it is obvious from the problem pages of many magazines that some people feel out of control about things happening in their life.

Out of control . . .

Some people feel that the world is out of control when they watch the news and see people being killed by earthquakes, and others slaughtered in war.

Crime figures show we are becoming a more violent society

Dear Jean,

I had to write, I have nobody else to talk to. My life seems to be going out of control. No one understands me and everything I do seems to go wrong . . . help!

630 die in earthquake

Study these extracts from newspapers and say why people sometimes feel things are out of control.

Someone in charge

Christians believe that God is in control of the world. They believe that God can be trusted even when things are scary and are going wrong. The biblical stories of creation point out that God created the world and that when he said something it was done. God said, 'Let there be light...' and there was light. What is more, it was good.

It is because Christians believe God is in control that they trust him. In the words of Father Yves Dubois, 'God has not gone on holiday and left us to it.' This does not mean that Christians have no problems—in fact, sometimes they have more problems because of their faith. However, their view of the world has been changed:

> 66 Believing that God created the world makes me feel safe. I know that it is not just an accident and that there is a reason behind the world. This means that my life has a purpose and meaning as part of that creation. 99
>
> KERSTIN, 16

Write a postcard home having just seen Rodin's sculpture. How would you describe it? What do you think Rodin is trying to say? What feelings come to mind when you look at it?

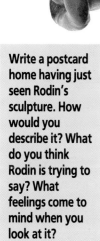

The French sculptor Rodin created this sculpture which he called 'The Hand of God.' The people are Adam and Eve.

Brain Engage

1 Write a description of a time when you have been really scared or felt really lost.

2 In the Bible find and read the following passages: Psalm 139:1–6; Matthew 6:26–34 and 10:29–31. What do these passages tell the believer about God's relationship to his creation?

3 Read the 'Dear Jean' letter on page 18. How might a Christian reply be different from a non-Christian reply? Write your own letter.

4 Choose a few words from one of the readings in (2) and use them to design a bookmark a Christian might have in his or her Bible. Illustrate your bookmark.

5 Look again at Rodin's sculpture. What picture would you use to show that God was someone to trust—who had the world in his hands? Draw it or write a poem.

Summary

Christians believe that God created the world and is in charge of it.

World on Loan

Summer holiday on planet earth

It is the year 2120. Planetary travel is all the rage. People have loads of places they can visit: Mars, Jupiter, Saturn... the sky's the limit! However, the earth is in danger of being deserted during the summer months.

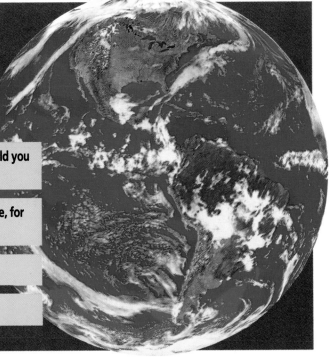

If you were working for a major holiday company, how would you get people to take their holidays on earth?

What good points would you highlight (a beautiful landscape, for example, or the progress of humanity)?

What would you have to 'keep quiet' about? Explain why.

Design the cover of your brochure.

This fragile earth

People's attitudes affect how they treat the world. Here are some reasons people give for dropping litter:

Somebody will pick it up— they're paid to.

Who cares anyway?

I forgot.

It's just a habit.

Xu Xi, aged 13, from China produced this dramatic picture, showing the need to protect the world from the threat of pollution.

What attitude might a gardener have about the world?

What attitude might a forestry worker have about the world?

What attitude might a property developer have about the world?

In the last few years 'green issues' have been headline news. Complete the following headlines to show how the incident affected the environment. For example: 'Shetland oil leak... kills thousands of sea birds.'

Untreated sewage...

Car fumes...

Rainforests...

- One animal species becomes extinct every half hour.
- In the Philippines 363 of the 412 rivers are polluted.
- The UK produces 23 million tonnes of rubbish each year.

1 When James Irwin stood on the moon and looked out at the earth, he described it as looking 'like a Christmas tree decoration'.

1a You are in space. Try to make up your own caption starting with 'The earth looks like . . .'

1b In groups draw a big globe and stick your captions on it. Display the work of the different groups so that you can see each other's globes.

2 Write a poem on attitudes to the earth. You could include the phrases 'World on Loan' and 'Rubbish Dump'.

3 Imagine it is the end of time, and God turns to the human race and wants to know what happened to the world he created—he has a few questions to ask us. What do you think he might want to say? Write an imaginary complaint from God. Use the following quotations from the Bible to get some idea of his nature and intentions: Genesis 1:28; Genesis 2:15; Psalm 8:4–9.

4 Some people say that Christians in the past have not taken environmental issues seriously enough. Do you think this is true? Should the church speak out more and make more of an effort? What could it do?

Rubbish dump, or gift from God?

Christians have a special interest in green issues. They believe that people are responsible to God for looking after the world and everything in it. They believe that the world is 'on loan' to us.

In the Bible's story of the creation of the world it says:

> 66 The Lord God took the man and put him in the garden of Eden to till it and look after it. 99
>
> GENESIS 2:15
> (REVISED ENGLISH BIBLE)

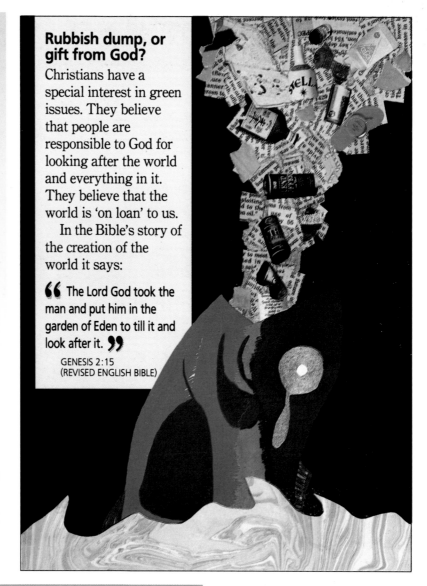

Waste and sewage pours into the sea every day, destroying life. Miho Uchida, from Japan, made this picture.

A Teenager's Prayer

Here is a prayer expressing the Christian view on creation:

> *Dear Lord,*
> *You created the environment for us to live in,*
> *the trees and grass, the blue sky and the*
>   *sparkling sea.*
> *You created it to provide homes and relationships,*
>   *yet we destroy the trees,*
> *we build factories where fields should be,*
> *we pollute the air with fumes,*
> *we dump our rubbish in the sea.*
> *God, we have turned the planet earth into a bomb of*
>   *another kind;*
> *not a bomb owned by the government*
> *but a bomb every person owns.*

 Extra

5 Find out about Francis of Assisi. Why is he famous? What was his attitude to creation?

 *Summary*

Christians believe that they are responsible for the care of the world. People are God's stewards.

That's Mine, I Made It!

Do you have something at home which you are really proud of because you made it yourself? In my bedroom I have a clay face which I made when I was at junior school. Although it is crumply and not very artistic it is special because I put so much effort into making it.

In groups make a list of things which are precious to you because you made them.

When we put so much effort into what we make or do we are proud of it. We get upset if other people don't recognize how important it is to us, and especially if it gets damaged. A piece of art tells us something about the person who puts so much energy into creating it. Poets have said that writing a poem is like giving birth to a baby! Perhaps you feel like that about your work.

'I feel a beautiful sense of closeness. My daughter is so dependent on me.'

A baby is a very special example of something humans create. Every baby is unique, and babies need continuing care and attention. Sometimes parents make big sacrifices.

Now my children have finished at college we can finally afford to go on holiday.

For the first two years of my daughter's life I existed on four hours of sleep each night.

Christians believe that God created the universe out of nothing and continues to take care of it. God didn't just design the world like a clock-maker who then lets the clock work itself. Instead, like a parent he continues to love and look after the world and everything in it, including people.

Brain Engage

1 Money isn't the only thing which a parent has to spend on a child. A lot more is involved. Write a job description for someone wanting to be a parent. Bring out how costly it will be, and what is expected of them.

2 Look up Colossians 1:15 and Hebrews 1:3. What do these two passages say about God's relationship to the world?

3a Look at the pictures on page 22. What do they tell you about people making things?

3b Christians talk about God making things. In what ways is the idea of God making things similar to humans making things? In what ways is it different?

4 Christians believe God cares for the world because he made it. Make a list of all the evidence a Christian might give to show that God cares. What might a person who doesn't believe in God say in reply? Compare your arguments with a friend. Discuss in class.

Summary

Christians believe that the Maker cares about his creation —he still looks after it.

Sam and the hacker

Here I Am is a book of imaginary conversations by Russell Stannard between Sam, a teenage computer buff, and God. God is referred to as 'the hacker' since he talks with Sam through his computer. In this extract Sam asks God what he is doing these days.

'Well,' I said, 'what are you doing these days---now that you're unemployed? Signing on at the Job Centre?'

'What? Sorry... I didn't get that...'

'Well, you created everything---got all this Universe going, right? So that's it. It just runs itself now. You aren't needed any more.'

'Not needed! You don't create a world and then just go on holiday! Who do you think stops the Universe from disappearing? Who keeps it in existence?

'Look, Sam,' said the hacker. 'I am into everything that exists. It's a bit like being an author. An author doesn't just write the first sentence of the story and then leave the rest to write itself...'

'Hold on. A story? What are you saying now? I'm just a character in a story---a story you've made up. Is that it?'

'In a way, yes. In good stories the characters come alive; they take on a life of their own. The author starts off thinking he'll make them do this, or do that---but then he realises such a person wouldn't do anything of the sort; they just wouldn't. So he has to give way; he has to write it differently. What comes out is a funny kind of mixture: what the author puts into it, but also what comes out of the characters themselves. Some characters are more famous than their authors. I enjoy being a character...'

'You? A character? But you just said you were the author. You can't be...'

'I'm both. I'm the Author of the story, but I'm also a character in the story. It's a story about me---living alongside people, working with them, sharing their troubles and joys...'

Where Did I Come From?

Different ways of explaining the same thing

The same thing can be described in different ways by different people. For example, a giant advertising billboard that lights up is described in one way by the electrician—who will give a careful explanation in electrical terms, so that we can understand just why and how each lamp is flashing—and in a completely different way by somebody who wants to know about the product being advertised. Both descriptions are right, in their own way.

Let's take another example—that of a kiss. How would you describe a kiss to somebody who had never had one? Here are two suggestions.

❝ A kiss is the exchange of microbes in the saliva of two people. This happens when there is physical contact of their lips. ❞

❝ A kiss makes two people feel like one. It is an expression of love. ❞

Who do you think they are written by?

Which do you think is the most accurate?

Which is the most meaningful explanation?

Rodin's sculpture 'The Kiss'.

We can see that descriptions differ because people are concentrating on different aspects. In the case of the kiss, one description is concerned with saying what is happening in purely biological terms whereas the other tries to explore the meaning, the importance of the kiss. In the same way when we look at questions about the beginning of life on earth we find that there are a number of explanations.

♀ Brain Engage

1 In groups make a list of things which can be described in two very different ways. Write out the descriptions. Mix up all the descriptions in a box. Take it in turns to pull out a description for the others to guess what it is.

2 You cannot measure the beauty of a sunset with a scientific instrument. Make a list of other things science cannot measure.

Genesis and science

The book of Genesis, in the Bible, tells the story of creation; science also offers information about how life on earth began. Because the two accounts are very different, it is often thought that if one is right, the other must be wrong—that we must choose between Genesis and science.

Genesis

The Bible teaches:

- The world was created by God in six 'days'. It is described as a series of great events taking place. However, in the Bible 'days' are not necessarily to be taken as 24-hour periods.

- Human beings are made 'in the image of God', different from all other creatures. Read for yourself Genesis 1—2:4a.

Science

Science says:

- The world probably began with a 'Big Bang'.

- Life on earth evolved. Some scientists believe that more complex animals, like humans, developed from earlier forms of animals, like the ape.

Genesis and science face us with some important questions:

- Can a person be a scientist and a Christian? Must we choose, or can both accounts be right?

- Are both accounts trying to do the same thing?

- Do they contradict or complement one another?

Two scientists explain how they understand both accounts:

66 Science and religion seek to answer different questions. Science asks how things happen, religion asks why. Genesis is not there to give us strict, technical answers about how the universe began. It gives us the big answer that things exist because of God's will. One can perfectly well believe in the Big Bang but [also] believe in it as the will of God the Creator. 99

JOHN POLKINGHORNE, PROFESSOR OF ASTRONOMY, CAMBRIDGE UNIVERSITY

66 In terms of evolution, we can get a scientific understanding of the mechanisms by which the earth and its life have come to be as we know them today, but it is beyond science to tell us why the world and humankind is as it is. 99

PROFESSOR BERRY, EVOLUTIONARY BIOLOGIST

Brain Engage

3 Design a poster which expresses the message 'God made this' using the story of creation in Genesis 1—2:4a.

Extra

4 Both Professor Berry and Professor Polkinghorne are scientists and Christians. Explain how they can believe in both the story of creation and the scientific account of the beginning of the world.

5 Using science books write a paragraph about: (a) the Big Bang (b) Evolution.

Summary

The Bible and science each offer an account of how the world began. Many Christians believe both accounts to be true.

Do I Count?

Am I just a number?

For a lot of the time many of us are just numbers to other people, numbers that come up on a computer screen when we hire out a video or sit an examination. In the past prisoners of war have had 'their number' tattooed upon their arms, just as cattle have numbers stamped on their skin.

Most people resent being treated like a statistic or code number. When two babies were born in a hospital the nursing staff made a terrible mistake, and mixed them up. It hit the newspaper headlines. Why? Because no two people are transferable. We all feel that each of us is unique and special. You can't just switch babies around like packs of sausages.

What would you feel if you picked up the wrong baby?

Christians believe that each person is more than just a number on a computer. They believe that each is unique and special. Human beings are different from all other animals. Our bodies and our personalities are unique, and we have a spiritual side too. The Bible says that 'God created human beings, making them to be like himself' (Genesis 1:27). Christians believe that each person has qualities which God also has. For example, they can be creative, and they are able to choose between right and wrong.

Christians believe that God values each person as a unique individual. His love for them began in the womb:

66 When my bones were being formed, carefully put together in my mother's womb, when I was growing there in secret, you [God] knew that I was there. 99

PSALM 139:15

1 The real me

1a Each of us is a 'one-off'; even twins are not duplicates of each other, they each have their own individuality. There are many things about us that other people do not see: feelings, secret thoughts and ideas. By yourself, write down the three most important things about the 'real' you. These may be things which only you know.

You might find the following questions useful:

- What makes you happiest?
- What makes you angry?
- What excites you?
- What bores you?
- How do you like to spend your spare time?

1b Now try to use these three things to write a poem using one of the following titles: 'Who Am I?' 'The Real Me Is . . .'

This is what one student wrote:

Who Am I?

I am my mind, my thoughts, my ideas.
I am my trust, my beliefs, my hopes.
I am my strengths, my weaknesses,
*   my understanding.*
I am one who loves, one who can be loved,
*   one who finds these things vital.*
I am part of the people around me; they
are part of me; I am one small piece of a
*   jigsaw.*
But most importantly I am myself—
I am one individual.

   GABI, 13

What makes one painting worth millions and another worth pennies? To my eyes they look no different. It's not the colour, the size, or the content. It's because one is original, like the Picasso shown here, and the other is a copy. But when it comes to people, there are no copies. Christians believe that each person 'bears God's signature'.

> 66 Very often I don't feel I am of any use to anybody but I know that to God I'm priceless. It's fantastic to be black because God made me this way and God doesn't make mistakes. 99
>
> ROSIE, UNEMPLOYED.

> 66 I see myself as special now, because I know God loves me, and because I know I am important to somebody. Now I can be myself, and be confident 99
>
> BETH

The Sculptor by Pablo Picasso © DACS 1995

Brain Engage

2 Spot the difference! Study the following headlines.

2a What is odd about the first two headlines?

2b What can you say about human beings from the other headlines?

2c Make a list of the ways in which human beings are different from animals.

2d Explain how this difference can be used for both good and bad purposes.

3 Read Psalm 8 and Luke 12:6–7. What do these two passages say about the value of human beings?

Poodle accused of murder

30 rabbits found worshipping God

Scientists are nearer finding a cure for AIDS

Leading researcher, David Hay, finds that 66% of humans are aware of God.

Summary

Christians believe that each person is a unique individual. Each person is of value because he or she is made 'in God's image'.

You're Amazing!

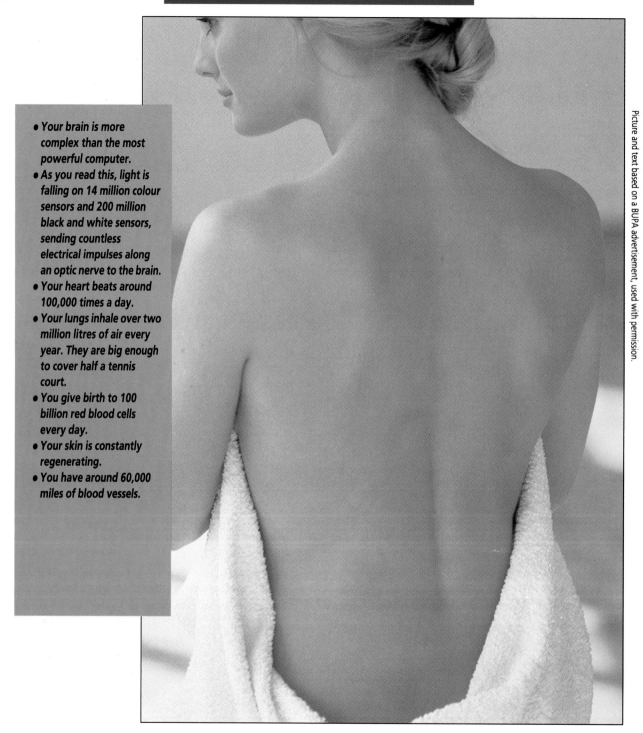

- Your brain is more complex than the most powerful computer.
- As you read this, light is falling on 14 million colour sensors and 200 million black and white sensors, sending countless electrical impulses along an optic nerve to the brain.
- Your heart beats around 100,000 times a day.
- Your lungs inhale over two million litres of air every year. They are big enough to cover half a tennis court.
- You give birth to 100 billion red blood cells every day.
- Your skin is constantly regenerating.
- You have around 60,000 miles of blood vessels.

Picture and text based on a BUPA advertisement, used with permission.

Did you know how amazing your body is? It might not feel like that on the day you wake up with a blocked nose, but that just shows how much we take for granted.

Christians believe that the human body is a special part of God's creation. The body is beautiful in itself, regardless of size and shape. After God had created human beings, he 'looked at everything he had made, and he was very pleased' (Genesis 1:31).

How do I look?

Do you like yourself? Do you ever say to yourself, 'if only I were thin, like…' or 'if only I had long straight hair, like…'? Everyone worries about how they look. A word has been invented to talk about the importance of looks to people. 'Lookism' stands for how people see themselves and how they are seen by others.

The media encourage lookism. Its effect can be enormous. For example some people, like the girl in the picture below, make themselves ill because they want to be an 'ideal shape'. The 'slimmer's disease', anorexia nervosa, is an extremely serious modern problem. It is estimated to affect one female in every hundred between the ages of 12 and 25.

The photograph of the sumo wrestler shows how people can abuse their bodies in a completely different way, by eating too much.

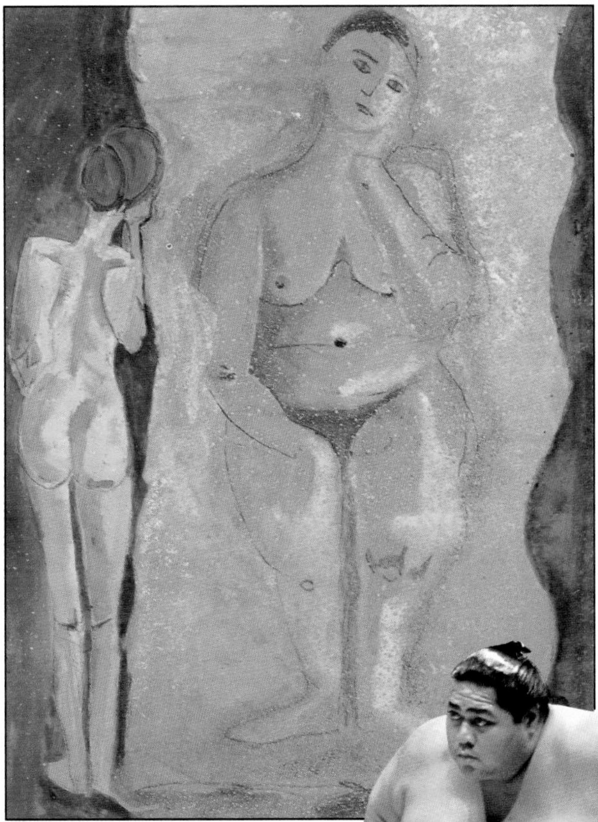

Christians believe that the body belongs to God, because it has been created by God. They believe that we have our bodies 'on loan' and need to respect and look after them properly.

What label would you give each of the pictures on this page?

What attitude(s) to the human body do you think each of the people in these pictures have?

What are you thinking as you look at these pictures?

List three other ways in which people abuse their bodies.

Why do they do it?

Brain Engage

1 Look again at the picture on the left-hand page. Under the title 'You're Amazing' write a list of things about yourself which you think are amazing. It may help you to think about the things you can do with your body (for example, see a butterfly or smell a flower).

2 To think about. Have you ever been criticized because of the way you look? Are looks important? Are you conscious of other people influencing how you feel you should look, what you should wear, how your hair should be cut? What is the image you have of the ideal body? What did you get this ideal from: parents, magazines, television, friends?

3 In what ways do you think the media encourage lookism? Search through old magazines and make a list of ways in which this is done. What is the type of ideal body they are presenting?

4 Write two pen-portraits of the perfect body:

4a from the viewpoint of a doctor

4b from the viewpoint of a body builder. How and why might these descriptions differ?

Summary

Christians believe that the human body is a wonderful part of God's creation. They believe that people should respect their bodies and not abuse them.

That's Not Fair!

Protestors clash during an anti-racist march in London.

Are men and women valued differently in society?

Are black and white people treated differently in today's world?

What do you think about (a) the unemployed, (b) people who earn very large wages? Is one group more important than the other? Explain.

60 out of 650 MPs are female

95% of top jobs go to men

A top male model can earn £3,000 a day. Top female model, Linda Evangelista, 27, earns £10,000 a day.

Brain Engage

1a Make two lists: one of what you think of as men's jobs and one of which you think are women's. Do you think it is right to distinguish between male and female jobs (what about a midwife)?

1b Research your favourite magazines to find out how women and men are presented. What value is attached to men/women in these magazines? Present your findings in a display.

1c How would you go about changing some of the stereotypes about men and women?

4 million unemployed people live off the state

You have been looking at the way society values people. Sometimes two people are treated completely differently, just because of the colour of their skin, or because of their sex. This leads to the comment, 'That's not fair!'

Christians believe that people should be treated equally because they are all equal in the eyes of God, whatever their race, sex or colour. They believe that each person—male or female, black or white, employed or unemployed—is created and loved by God.

❝ There is no difference between Jews and Gentiles, between slaves and free men, between men and women; you are all one in union with Christ Jesus. ❞

GALATIANS 3:28

Christians believe that people are born equal but different. This is especially true of the sexes—equal but different, complementing one another. In Christian marriage God is involved in uniting two people who will complement each other: they promise to love and remain faithful to each other for life.

Anna explains why she wants to get married:

❝ What does marriage mean? It means giving up at least a little part of ourselves to another person. It means a certain sacrifice, selflessness in the true nature of the word. However, the fashion today is to live together. Why? Because we don't want responsibilities. To reject marriage can involve the rejection of a certain kind of relationship between people. In my opinion it means that there is much more selfishness and fear. ❞

Brain Engage

2 Write a letter to either Graham or Anna. Start with the words, 'Dear Anna/Graham, I would like to comment on some of the things you say . . .' Continue the letter mentioning in what ways you agree and/or disagree with her/him.

Extra

3a Discuss the following statements. In each case write two arguments for and two arguments against the statement.

- 'If we make a mistake it doesn't matter because we can always get divorced.'
- 'People want too much from marriage.'
- 'Why get married? It's better to live together.'

3b Explain how a Christian would reply to these statements.

Graham explains why it was important for him and Pippa to get married in church:

❝ When we got married, God was very much involved. He was and is the unseen third partner of the marriage. The closer I move towards God the closer I move towards Pippa. Marriage is something we have to work hard at, it is not always easy. Marriage is about each of us respecting each other's individuality. It is about helping the other person become the person they are meant to be. It is not about one being boss over the other. We are both equal. God is with us, helping us to grow together. ❞

Summary

Christians believe that although we are all different, each person is of equal value. This is reflected in the marriage ceremony where two equal people agree to complement each other for the rest of their lives.

Do I, Don't I?

How are human beings different from computers?

One basic difference is that people can think for themselves; they are not robots. They are free to make their own decisions. However, being able to make choices is not always easy. It can bring people into conflict with each other.

Christians believe that when God created people he did not want robots. They were given free will to make their own choices. Christians believe that people are held responsible for the choices they make in life. In the Bible Paul wrote that all people have the law of God 'written on their hearts' (Romans 2:15), though from the very beginning people have shown a tendency to make wrong choices.

Write your own caption to this picture.

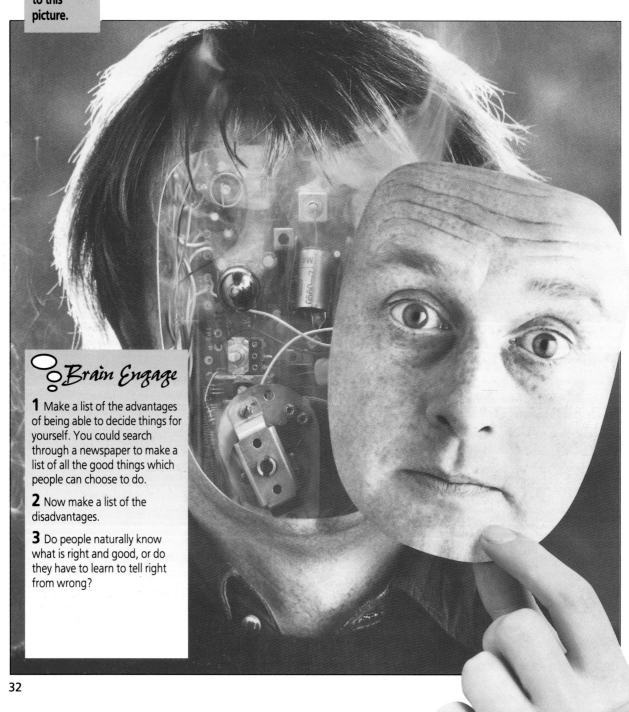

Brain Engage

1 Make a list of the advantages of being able to decide things for yourself. You could search through a newspaper to make a list of all the good things which people can choose to do.

2 Now make a list of the disadvantages.

3 Do people naturally know what is right and good, or do they have to learn to tell right from wrong?

Yes, I will, no, I won't: the moral maze

In groups decide what you would do in the following situations:

Brain Engage

4 As a class make a list of:

4a situations in which you have to use your free will.

4b situations in which adults have to use their free will, for example issues such as euthanasia.

4c global situations in which nations have to use their free will, for example whether or not to go to war.

5 How would you answer somebody who asked, 'Why didn't God programme us to do good?'

1: Job at stake
It's Friday afternoon. You work as a volunteer at the old people's home from 6 to 9 o'clock. However, a friend has just rung up inviting you to a party. What do you do?

2: Harmless fun
Your parents have gone away for the weekend and a friend has come to stay. Your parents told you before they left that you were not to have people round when they were out. Your friend suggests that you have a small party. It can't do any harm and no one will know. What do you do?

3: Opportunity knocks
The teacher has left the class. She has made the mistake of leaving the next day's test papers on her desk. What do you do?

Summary

Christians believe that God created people with the freedom to choose between good and bad.

The Dark Side of Life

Why are we fascinated with video nasties, horror films, and torture? Why do people do what they know is wrong—bullying, for example?

What is bullying?

Bullies set out to get some hold over others and make them feel ashamed, unhappy or afraid.

They may hurt their victims

- physically (for example, kicking or punching)
- verbally (for example, by teasing, name-calling, threatening somebody)
- emotionally (for example, by deliberately ignoring somebody).

Bullying may go on for months or even years, making the victim's life a misery.

Why do people bully others?

Boys often bully in order to show their power over others. Girls often bully in order to be part of a group and to keep others out of their friendship group.

Victim of schoolboy bullies hanged himself

A boy aged 12 was found hanged with his brother's school tie after becoming the victim of playground bullies. An inquest in Birmingham was told yesterday that Stephan had been menaced by demands to hand over his tuckshop money. The bullies had told him, 'Bring us some money every day or we will punch your head in.'

From The Times, Thursday 14 October 1993.

Look at the photo. Imagine that it was going to be used as a poster against bullying. What caption would you add to it?

I don't watch the news any more. I find it too depressing to see people's inhumanity to each other day after day.

Why are we nasty?

In a survey four sixteen-year-old students suggested the following reasons for doing things they knew were wrong.

> “I'm made like that. I'm an angry person. Life's not been good to me, so why should I be good to it?”
>
> JAMES

> “It's good fun. There's no excitement in being a goody-goody. If you were good all the time life would be boring.”
>
> NATASHA

> “It's my parents' fault. They taught me everything I know!”
>
> JULIA

> “I get tempted to do these things, like a voice inside my head.”
>
> JUSTIN

Which of these do you think is most convincing?

Justify your choice by writing a paragraph supporting your view.

Which is the least convincing? Why?

The human disease

The truth is we don't need to be taught to be nasty, it just seems to come naturally. It is like a cancer which is inside us all.

In the Bible, Jesus diagnoses this disease:

> “From the inside, from a person's heart, come the evil ideas which lead him to do immoral things, to rob, kill, commit adultery, be greedy, and do all sorts of evil things.”
>
> MARK 7:21

St Paul struggled with it:

> “I do not understand what I do;
> for I don't do what I would like to do,
> but instead I do what I hate.”
>
> ROMANS 7:15

Christians call this disease SIN. It is not just doing wrong things. It is a bias deep within people to do what is wrong. Sin is like a disease that needs curing. We will never be rid of it otherwise. Like cancer, unless it is treated it will take over the whole person.

Brain Engage

1a List the top five things you think people of your age are tempted to do.

1b Which of these is the worst and darkest?

1c What would a Christian view on this be?

2 Does everyone know the difference between right and wrong? Where does this knowledge come from? Discuss your ideas.

3 Draw a picture to represent the 'struggle' inside us all—the struggle between the temptation to do wrong and the knowledge that we should do what is right (a magnet is one idea you could use).

4 Make a list of words and phrases which people associate with wrongdoing in us. Find an alternative or opposite word for each one. For example: mean—generous.

What the Bible teaches

The Bible says that the root of the problem is people's rebellion against God. In Genesis chapter three the Bible tells the story of the Fall (see page 38). People understand this story in different ways but the message is clear: God the Creator gave people the freedom to choose good or evil. They chose to go their own way instead of obeying God, with terrible consequences.

Summary

Christians believe that people have a bias to do wrong. They look back to the Bible's story of the Fall of Adam and Eve as a way of explaining how the world God made was spoiled.

A Traitor in the Camp

Sometimes the wrong things that people do are so horrendous that the word 'evil' is used to describe them. This word was used of the two ten-year-old boys who brutally murdered two-year-old James Bulger.

DAILY RECORD

Mr. Justice Morland told Robert Thompson and Jon Venables: 'What you did was evil and brutal. Your conduct was both cunning and wicked.'

In the 17-day trial the jury heard how little James was abducted from his mother in a Liverpool shopping centre. They took him on an exhausting two-mile journey to his death. On a dark, lonely railway track, bricks were thrown at the frightened child, a heavy metal bar was hurled on to his head and he was punched, kicked and stamped on. His tiny body was left to be cut in two by a train.

Police believe the worst aspects of both children's characters combined to kill.

THURSDAY 25 NOVEMBER, 1993

What is evil?

Some theologians say that 'evil' can be seen in a number of areas:

- personal: as in the James Bulger case

- social: homelessness, deprivation

- institutional: when people are exploited in organizations like industry—or school!

During the trial various reasons were given as to why these two boys murdered James.

The father of one of the two boys had been watching a horror movie called *Child's Play 3* which echoed the terrifying details of James' murder. The video shows the gruesome death of a boy doll on a railway track. The police discovered that he had hired a total of 440 films, many of which were 'video nasties'.

Jon Venables' mum blamed his school, social workers, neighbours and the police for failing to keep track of her child. She admitted that her son is 'a little liar, he's devious, he's a scally, he robs, he plays truant'.

Is this the whole story? The newspaper headline reflects the judge's comment that there was more to it than that. These two boys were called 'evil'. What does it mean to call somebody evil?

> Draw a small diagram with a person in the middle. Around this figure indicate all the evil influences (personal, social and institutional) at work on the one hand and all the good that can influence them on the other. You could use arrows and words or draw pictures to illustrate these.

Sometimes whole periods of history seem given over to evil. One example was the Holocaust in the Second World War. Hitler blamed the Jews for all the things which were going wrong in Germany at the time. He thought that they were sub-human and set out to destroy them. In 1941 Hitler devised the Final Solution to the Jewish 'problem': they were sent to concentration camps where the strongest worked as slaves. Many died from disease. The large majority were gassed to death. Six million Jews were killed.

Brain Engage

1 Divide a page in two down the middle. On one side list examples of evil and wrongdoing you might hear of in one day. On the other side list examples of good, kind and generous activities that go on around you in the world without hitting the news. Set out a newspaper page using these examples.

2 Here are three people:

- Jeff, who believes evil is caused by the devil.
- Lucy, who believes evil is social.
- Alan, who believes you are born with it.

Get into groups of three. Choose a part to take, either Jeff, Lucy or Alan. Discuss the James Bulger case from your point of view.

Extra

3 Prepare for a class debate on the motion: 'This class believes that the devil exists.' Choose to support or oppose this statement and write your speech.

Where does this evil come from?

While Christians believe that people have the freedom to choose between right and wrong, they also believe there is an evil agent at work in the world. The Bible calls this evil force the devil or Satan. Christians believe that God's plans are for goodness and peace, and the devil works to cause suffering and destruction.

Cartoonists often poke fun when they draw the devil. However, Christians believe that behind these pictures is a reality which should be taken seriously. After all, war cartoonists poked fun at Hitler but people still took him very seriously.

Ideas from the Bible

The Bible tells how Satan works to turn people away from God.

- It was the devil who tempted Adam and Eve to turn against God (Genesis 3).
- After Jesus was baptized he was tempted by the devil to use his power for himself and to rebel against God (Luke 4:1–13).

- Jesus showed his power over the devil when he carried out exorcisms and cast out demons (for example Mark 5:1–20).
- The Bible looks forward to a time when the devil will be completely defeated, when Jesus returns to judge the world.

Summary

Christians believe that evil exists—that the devil is at work in the world.

I Can Resist Anything But Temptation!

The Bible says that the central problem with humanity is its rebellion against God. It tells a story to show how people were tempted to disobey him and gave in to the temptation: they decided to do what they wanted. The story can be found in Genesis 3:1–24. It is sometimes called the story of the Fall.

Which part of the story does this painting by Massaccio illustrate?

What do you think are the feelings of Adam and Eve in this picture?

Why do you think that it is sometimes called the story of the Fall? What are the people falling from?

People understand this story in different ways:

Brain Engage

1 Adam and Eve
(a) Who tempted Adam and Eve? (b) What were Adam and Eve tempted to do? (c) What was Adam and Eve's response to God? (d) What were the consequences of their disobediences? (e) What happened to Adam and Eve's relationship to God?

2 Act out the story of Adam and Eve. It is a story about temptation. If you want, you can put it in a modern setting. You must include the following characters: Adam, Eve, the serpent, God, the narrator. Make it humorous, if you like, but bring out the central theme of temptation.

3 What do you think Nathan means when he says that 'the story explains a lot about God and people'? Suggest three things which it explains.

Extra

4 Many popular magazines have problem pages where people write in to ask for advice on things going wrong in their lives.

4a Select two or three problems from a recent problem page. What is at the root of the problem?

4b Do you think that the Christian teaching in the story of the Fall helps to explain the cause of the problem? Explain your response.

66 Adam and Eve were as real as Madonna and the Queen because it's written in the Bible. 99

MARSHA, 16

66 Adam, Eve and the Garden of Eden did not really exist, but that doesn't make the story untrue. The story explains a lot about God and people. 99

NATHAN, 15

66 There can't have been a real Adam and Eve. After all if they were our first parents where did all the different colours of people come from? 99

JASON, 17

Where does temptation come from?

We have already seen that people give a number of answers to this question (see pages 34–35).

The Screwtape Letters

C.S. Lewis held the traditional Christian belief that the devil was a reality and that his main task was to take control of people's thoughts and actions without them knowing it. In Lewis' book *The Screwtape Letters* a junior devil called Wormwood writes to his uncle, Screwtape, with reports of his attempts to tempt people to do wrong. Uncle Screwtape writes back with his comments.

see pages 34–35

My dear Wormwood,
  I am very pleased by what you tell me about this man's relations with his mother. When two humans have lived together for many years it usually happens that each has tones of voice and expressions of face which are almost unendurably irritating to the other. Work on that. Bring fully into the consciousness of your patient that particular lift of his mother's eyebrows which he learned to dislike in the nursery, and let him think how much he dislikes it. Let him assume that she knows how annoying it is and does it to annoy. And, of course, never let him suspect that he has tones and looks which similarly annoy her. As he cannot see or hear himself, this is easily managed. In civilised life domestic hatred usually expresses itself by saying things which would appear quite harmless on paper (the words are not offensive) but in such a voice, or at such a moment, that they are not far short of a blow in the face. You know the kind of thing: 'I simply ask her what time dinner will be and she flies into a temper.' Keep this game up.
    Your affectionate uncle,
    Screwtape

The plot of the *Letters* is not concerned with big issues. Instead, Lewis concentrates on the really trivial things in life, like the tone of voice or the lift of the eyebrow. He knew that it is these things which cause the most rows and troubles between people. Here is where real temptation lies.

ꝍ Brain Engage

5 Write your own Screwtape Letter. First choose what your temptation is going to be. Why is it so tempting? Then imagine that you are a junior devil tempting someone to give way to the temptation. Write a report back to your uncle Screwtape. However, you must bear the following rules in mind:

- unlike God the devil is not all-powerful. Screwtape relies on others to give him information: he is not all seeing and knowing.

- the devil can only work where there is a human will for him to control.

Summary

Christians believe that people are constantly tempted to give in to selfishness and to do wrong. They also believe that the devil is a powerful agent in this.

Rescue Operation

Skier's mountainside rescue

An injured skier was rescued yesterday in a dramatic mountainside helicopter operation. Flying in hazardous conditions across the frozen Alps, they raced against time to save an experienced skier who had sustained life-threatening injuries in a high speed fall.

The skier, Pierre Mahaud, 29, was air-lifted to hospital where a spokesperson has described his condition as 'comfortable'.

Jesus the rescuer

The Christian faith is centred on Jesus. The name has a special meaning: 'Jesus' (in Hebrew) means 'God rescues'. We have seen how sin can be thought of as a deadly disease. The Bible also teaches that sin separates people from God. No way can human badness mix with God's goodness. They are poles apart. Christians believe that human beings are like the skier injured on the mountainside. They need to be rescued. Christians believe that God loves his world so much that he sent Jesus on a rescue mission—one that cost him his life.

Rescuing the lost

Jesus told three parables to illustrate how he had come to rescue the lost. One of them was the **parable of the lost sheep** (Luke 15:1–7).

The story goes like this:

A shepherd has a hundred sheep and loses one of them. He leaves the other ninety-nine and goes looking for the one that was lost. When he finds it he is so happy that he puts it on his shoulders and carries it back home. He calls together his neighbours and friends and celebrates the fact that he has found the sheep which was lost.

What is special about this story?

Jesus is like the shepherd who cares for every individual sheep. Jesus came to rescue people who have lost their way to God. When he finds each person he celebrates their return to God.

The other stories he told to illustrate the same point are the story of the lost coin (Luke 15:8–10) and the story of the lost son (Luke 15:11–32).

Light to the rescue

Some rescue operations need search lights to find mountaineers caught in the darkness of a foggy night. Christians use the symbol of light to show that Jesus came to rescue people from the darkness of all that cuts them off from God. Jesus called himself 'the Light of the World' (John 8:12). At the beginning of his Gospel account John describes Jesus as 'the real light that comes into the world and shines on all mankind' (John 1:9).

It only takes one light to put out the darkness.

Advent

For many Christians Christmas preparations start four Sundays before Christmas, at the beginning of the season of Advent. The word 'advent' means coming or arrival. It is the time of the year when Christians get ready for the coming of Jesus.

The Advent crown

An Advent crown is a circle of four candles decorated with holly and ribbons. The first candle is lit on the first Sunday of Advent, two candles on the second, and so on until all are alight on the Sunday before Christmas. As the time until Christmas gets shorter the light from the Advent crown increases.

Brain Engage

1 Rescue stories often capture the headlines. Why do you think people like rescue stories? What makes a good rescue story? Discuss in pairs and share your ideas with the class.

2 Imagine that you were the rescued skier being interviewed by a journalist. He asks you to describe the feelings you had: (a) stranded on the mountain; (b) when you were rescued. Write what you would say to him.

3 Design an introductory screen image that would come at the beginning of a TV serial called 'God's rescue programme'.

4 Design a stained-glass window based on the story of the lost sheep. You should attempt to bring out the meaning of the story.

5 Read through the text on these pages. Pick out those words and phrases which tell you something about what Christians believe about God and his work in the world.

Extra

6 Write a poem about Advent, bringing out the meaning of this season. In it you should use the words 'rescue' and 'light'.

Summary

Christians believe Jesus was sent by God to rescue (save) people from sin: 'For us and for our salvation he came down from heaven' (Apostles' Creed).

A Special Birth

Every human birth is special to parents. However, Christians believe that one particular birth was even more special. It was special because the baby was Jesus, believed by Christians to be the 'Son of God': God himself in human form. The Bible tells of an angel's message to Mary, a young woman—a virgin—living in Nazareth (in present-day Israel) that she had been chosen to be the mother of this special child. There are two accounts of this event, one in the Gospel of Matthew, one in the Gospel of Luke.

People often speak of the birth of a baby as a 'miracle' or a 'mystery'. Why do you think they feel these words are the right ones?

Look at the photos. What words would you choose to talk about the special event of a birth? Write them into a poem called 'Birth'.

Ask your mum and/or dad to tell you anything they remember about your birth. We usually remember the details of days when very important things happen. What do your parents remember about your birth day?

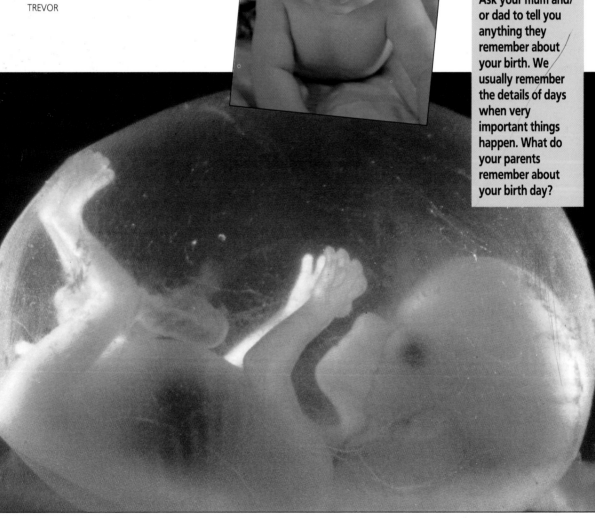

Read the two accounts of Jesus' birth. Split a page in half. In one column write Matthew 1:18—2:12. In the other write Luke 2: 1–20. Under each title make a list of things which happen in each account of the birth of Jesus. How are they the same? How do they differ?

What aspects of the story tell us that the writers want us to understand that this was no ordinary birth?

A baby is a helpless, weak and vulnerable creature, yet the baby Jesus is an important image for Christians. What does it tell you about the Christian view of God?

The Nativity Play

At Christmas many young children act out the events of that first Christmas in nativity plays ('nativity' means 'birth').

The first such play took place on Christmas Eve 1223 when Francis of Assisi and his followers climbed the rocky hillside above their village of Greccio in Italy, and prepared a manger. Local people came to join them, carrying burning torches to light up the night. Ox and ass were led in and the joy and hardships of Jesus' birth were acted out. As the villagers watched, St Francis began to tell the story of the first Christmas, taking the part of each character in turn. Francis' aim in life was to live as Jesus did. He was determined that ordinary men and women should understand what it meant for God's Son to be born poor, in a place where animals were sheltered.

Brain Engage

1 Prepare a 'rap' under the title 'No ordinary birth' for presenting in a special Christmas assembly.

2 Have we lost the real meaning of Christmas? Look at Christmas celebrations—how much is linked to the original meaning? Make a survey of Christmas cards. Group them according to subject matter. What do you notice? Why?

3 Value auction: List all the things people in your class think are important about Christmas. They have £100 to buy five things from that list for a happy Christmas. Organize the auction. Work in pairs and list the things you are going to bid for before the auction begins. You will need a reserve list. What essential things of Christmas cannot be bought/auctioned?

Epiphany

Matthew's Gospel tells of three visitors from the East who brought gifts to Jesus soon after his birth. Today Christians still celebrate the coming of these three to visit Jesus (Matthew 2:1–12) on the feast of Epiphany (6 January). 'Epiphany' is a word which means 'to make obvious', 'to reveal'. The visitors recognized Jesus as the true King and Saviour, the rescuer of the world. They showed the importance of Jesus by the gifts they gave him:

- gold, a gift for kings

- frankincense, a sweet-smelling incense used in worship: it was to show that Jesus is to be worshipped

- myrrh, a spice that was used to prepare dead bodies for burial; this gift is seen as foretelling that Jesus, the rescuer, had to die in order to save the world.

Summary

Christians believe that Jesus was God's Son: 'We believe in one Lord Jesus Christ, the only Son of God' (Apostles' Creed).

Days of Destiny

Jesus started his main work when he was about thirty years old. It lasted for three years. When the Gospel writers came to write about his life, certain events stood out for them as being of special importance. These events pointed to who Jesus was and what he had come to do.

● **SNAPSHOT 1: Jesus' baptism**

❝ Jesus came from Nazareth in the province of Galilee and was baptized by John in the Jordan. As soon as Jesus came up out of the water, he saw heaven opening and the Spirit coming down on him like a dove. And a voice came from heaven, 'You are my own dear Son. I am pleased with you.' ❞

MARK 1:9–11

This was a key moment in Jesus' life. God had called him for a specific job. Mark says that God then sent him into the desert, to prepare for the task he had to do.

> What does this story tell us about who Jesus was?

● **SNAPSHOT 2: Temptation in the desert**

❝ Jesus was led by the Spirit into the desert, where he was tempted by the Devil for forty days. In all that time he ate nothing, so that he was hungry when it was over. ❞

LUKE 4

The Gospels record three specific temptations.

1 Jesus was tempted to misuse his God-given power to satisfy his own needs.

❝ The Devil said to him, 'If you are God's Son, order this stone to turn into bread.' But Jesus answered, 'The scripture says, "Man cannot live on bread alone." ' ❞

2 Jesus was tempted by the offer of power and wealth:

❝ Then the Devil took him up and showed him in a second all the kingdoms of the world. 'I will give you all this power and all this wealth,' the Devil told him... 'All this will be yours, then, if you worship me.' Jesus answered, 'The scripture says, "Worship the Lord your God and serve only him!" ' ❞

3 Jesus was tempted to test his powers by a public display to impress the world.

❝ Then the Devil took him to Jerusalem and set him on the highest point of the Temple, and said to him, 'If you are God's Son, throw yourself down from here.' ... But Jesus answered, 'The scripture says, "Do not put the Lord your God to the test." ' ❞

LUKE 4:1–13

Jesus was tempted in the same way as other human beings, and yet he did not give in. He refused to misuse the special gifts God had given him by using his power for his own ends. He chose instead to do things God's way.

> Do the temptations stress the human nature of Jesus or his nature as God's son?

● SNAPSHOT 3: Transfiguration

After his baptism and the temptations, Jesus began to teach. He attracted many followers, and from these chose twelve to be his close friends. The next key event took place after they had been with him some time, hearing his teaching and seeing him heal many sick people. Three of Jesus' disciples were given a special insight into who Jesus was.

> ❝ Jesus took Peter, John, and James with him and went up a hill to pray. While he was praying, his face changed its appearance, and his clothes became dazzling white. Suddenly two men were there talking with him. They were Moses and Elijah, who appeared in heavenly glory and talked with Jesus about the way in which he would soon fulfil God's purpose by dying in Jerusalem. Peter and his companions were sound asleep, but they woke up and saw Jesus' glory and the two men who were standing with him ... a cloud appeared and covered them with its shadow ... A voice said from the cloud, 'This is my Son, whom I have chosen—listen to him!' When the voice stopped, there was Jesus all alone. ❞
>
> LUKE 9:28–36

- The disciples are given a glimpse of Jesus as the Son of God, but ...
- Jesus has to die in order to fulfil God's purpose.

○ Brain Engage

1 Jesus was chosen for a special task at his baptism. Baptism was a turning-point in Jesus' life. Describe a turning-point in your life or that of someone you know. Explain what happened and how life changed afterwards.

2a Jesus was tempted to misuse his power. What does the word 'temptation' mean? Look through a newspaper to find stories of people who abuse their power.

2b Jesus was able to triumph over temptation. What helped him to answer the devil and what qualities do you think he possessed that made this possible?

2c Imagine that Jesus was alive on earth now. How do these temptations relate to temptations in everyone's life? What would be the temptations of the present age: to use his power for himself; to build his own empire, not God's; to use his power to impress the world? Tell the story in the form of a newspaper front page.

3 Transfiguration. You are a TV reporter. You approach Peter, John and James. What questions would you ask? What research would you have to do to make sense of this story?

From the time of the transfiguration, Jesus began to prepare his followers for his death. This scene from the film *Jesus of Nazareth* shows his triumphal entry into Jerusalem, when the crowds went wild. Five days later, the mob howled for his death, and he was crucified.

*S*ummary

Christians believe that Jesus was really human, yet shared God's nature too.

Super Hero

How would you describe these computer heroes? What qualities do they have?

In groups make a list of the qualities you look for in a hero. For example, do they have to be good-looking, successful, strong?

Jesus: the hero who . . .

Within two generations of Jesus' death four portraits of his life were written. Each writer was writing for a purpose, not just writing a book about Jesus' life, like a biography.

These four portraits are called 'Gospels', a word which means 'good news'. Each of the four Gospel writers believed that Jesus and his teaching about God was *good news*, that in Jesus God had come close to people. For each writer, Jesus was the hero. The Gospel writers show how people left their homes and jobs to follow him; how his enemies thought his influence so dangerous that they had to get rid of

him. Although they wrote the story after Jesus' death, they were convinced that Jesus was alive, and that he still called people to follow him.

Each of the Gospels provides a slightly different portrait of Jesus. The authors wrote in their own distinctive ways, in order to provide the key to Jesus' importance. The Gospels show what the first Christians understood about who Jesus was. The writers say very little about the first thirty years of his life. They focus on just a few years of public activity, and they give almost a quarter of the space in their books to describing the events leading up to and surrounding his death.

Hero profiles

1 Luke: Jesus, friend of the outcast

She's a real pain

Don't touch him, you might catch germs

She's really ugly

He's dirty

2 John: Jesus as the Son of God

John's Gospel stresses the fact that Jesus himself possesses, and shows us, the nature of God. John opens his Gospel by calling Jesus the 'Word of God' who 'was God' (John 1:1). Instead of telling about Jesus' birth, John begins by explaining that he was with God from before the creation of the universe. Only John spells out Jesus' claim to be 'one' with his heavenly Father. In this Gospel, Thomas, one of the twelve disciples, touches the risen Jesus and says, 'My Lord and my God' (20:29). Only John records seven remarkable claims which Jesus made about himself, all starting with the words 'I am...': 'I am the Light of the world' (8:12); '... I am the Way, the Truth and the Life' (14:6); 'I am the Resurrection and the Life' (11:25).

Although John stresses the 'God side' of Jesus' nature he also makes his human nature clear when he writes that 'The Word became flesh and made his dwelling among us' (John 1:14). God truly became fully human in the person of Jesus of Nazareth.

Have you ever heard things like this said about people? These are the people no one wants to know, the 'outcasts'.

In Luke's Gospel Jesus is shown over and over again as someone who really cares about those who are rejected by society. He takes special trouble over them. At the time of Jesus these 'outcasts' included the Gentiles (non-Jews), Samaritans (half-Jew, half-Gentile), tax collectors (seen as traitors who supported Rome), the poor, the lepers, the prostitutes and women generally.

Following the example of Jesus, The Salvation Army cares for London's homeless.

What Jesus said to 'outcasts':

To a woman who lived an immoral life:

66 Your sins are forgiven... go in peace. 99

LUKE 7: 48–50

To Levi the tax collector:

66 Follow me. 99

LUKE 5:27

66 I believe that Jesus was closer to a gypsy than we are: he never used to call a town his own. I believe that Jesus was closer to showing us our way of life to what anyone else was. 99

ROY TAYLOR, TRAVELLER

Brain Engage

1 Compare the hero-image you described at the beginning of the page with what Luke and John say about Jesus.

2 Although people can't actually become invisible, many people (for example the old trapped in their own homes) feel they are invisible to others. Make a list of other 'invisible people' in today's society: in your school, your community, the country.

3 What was Jesus' attitude to these 'invisible people'? Find the following passages in Luke's Gospel to help you write a paragraph: Luke 5:12–14: the man with leprosy; Luke 19: 1–10: the tax collector; Luke 7:36–50: the woman leading a sinful life.

Extra

4 Imagine that you had to prepare a television programme about John's picture of Jesus.

4a What difficulties would you have?

4b How would you present the 'God side' of Jesus' nature?

Summary

Each of the four Gospels presents a 'window' into understanding who Jesus was.

The Human Face of God

As Jesus' first followers thought about the life of Jesus they came to believe that he was more than a human being. He was God's Son who came and lived as a man on earth. Matthew gave Jesus the name 'Emmanuel' which means 'God is with us'—God has come to earth. That is why Christmas, the celebration of his birth, is such an important day in the church calendar. When asked 'what is God like?'

Christians point to Jesus. He is the human face of God.

Artists have often tried to paint pictures which express the belief that Jesus was both fully human and fully God. Here are two of them:

Look at each picture and decide if it stresses the 'God side' or the 'human side' of Jesus.

Carefully look at both pictures. Make a list of words which express your feelings as you look at them. You may like to choose from the following, but also try to add your own: kind, painful, compassionate, tearful, sad, holy, peaceful, uncomfortable.

What does it mean to say Jesus was fully human?

When Christians say that God became human in Jesus they are saying that he experienced human thoughts, feelings, talents, temptations, pain. Even though he was God he knows exactly what it is like to be human. The one difference was that Jesus never felt guilt because he never did wrong.

The cost of becoming a human being

Christians believe that Jesus was God's gift to the world. Jesus was his Father's way of showing how much he loved people. The following story explores the fact that unselfish love can be very costly.

John and his mother's hands

It was not until John was twelve that he really noticed his mother's hands. Although she was in every other way a beautiful woman her hands were scarred and twisted. John's father was the first to notice that something was wrong: John no longer brought his friends home.

One day his father asked him what was wrong, why didn't he bring his friends home anymore? John replied that there was no real reason. 'Is it anything to do with your mum's hands?' his father asked. John went bright red, but remained silent. 'Perhaps you would like to know how your mother got all those scars, because they were beautiful hands when I married her?' John didn't say anything and so his father went on.

He told John how one day when he was a toddler he had run into the living room and got too close to the fire. 'Your clothes caught fire. You screamed, mum rushed in, and because there was nothing else available she smothered the fire with her own hands. She saved you but sacrificed her hands in doing so.'

John couldn't say a word, but after a few days he started to bring friends back home. From then onwards he always made a point of asking his friends very discreetly to note his mother's hands. 'You see,' he would say, 'she burnt them because she loved me so much.'

Brain Engage

1 Write a letter 'to whom it may concern' (or God) which describes what is hard about being a human being.

2 Write a list of questions you want to ask God about becoming a human being—why did he do it? What did it feel like? Try to think out the answers that God would give from what you have learnt here.

3 Look up the following references to find out how the early Christians came to speak about Jesus:
A real human being (1 Timothy 2:5, Hebrews 2:14–18)
Son of God (Mark 1:11; 9:7; Matthew 11:27; Matthew 16:16-17; Galatians 4:4; Hebrews 1:1–3).

4 John's Gospel begins with a poem which attempts to describe how God became a human being. Read it for yourself (John 1:1–18). Make a list of statements showing what this poem says about Jesus.

God is with us

Peter (18) explains why it is important for him that God became a human being:

66 I wasn't brought up in a religious home, and for many years the whole religious business seemed so irrelevant to my life. I needed people who could understand what I was going through—the good things in life like sharing a joke, having a drink with friends. Also people who knew what it was like to feel low and unhappy. Then, one Christmas I was watching this film on the TV about Jesus. As I watched I started to realize that this man did know everything about what I was going through. He knew what it was to be happy and also being miserable. He knew what it is to be lonely, to suffer and to face death. From that moment onwards I knew I could trust someone who knew more about life than I did. 99

When Christians talk about God becoming a human being in Jesus they use the word 'incarnation'. The word means 'in the flesh', and refers to the belief that God took on not just human form, but a real body—flesh and blood—when Jesus was born.

Summary

Christians believe that God became a real human being in Jesus. This belief is called the *incarnation*.

It's All Gone Wrong!

Rescue the runaway

Jesus told a story about someone who ran away from home, when he wanted people to understand what had happened between God and people. The story goes like this:

The runaway son: Luke 15:11–32

- There was a man who had two sons. His property would be divided between them when he died.

- The younger son wanted his share to enjoy now, so his father gave him the money.

- The son left home and lived it up, spending everything.

- But then a famine hit the country. The son was so desperate for food that he went to work on a pig farm.

- Eventually he decided to go home, say he'd been wrong, and ask his father to take him back. He was frightened what his father would say.

- But when he got in sight of home his father ran to meet him and welcomed him with open arms.

- His father organized the best party he could for his younger son because he was so glad he had come back. The elder son, who had stayed working on his father's farm, was dreadfully jealous. But his father told him to celebrate and be happy, 'because your brother was lost, but now he has been found'.

What to notice about the story

- The father represents God. The sons represent everyone.

- The Jews, Jesus' own nation, were commanded by God to respect their parents. The Law would have punished this kind of rebellion by stoning the son to death (Deuteronomy 21:18–21).

- The younger son left home because he wanted to live his own life according to his own rules, although this meant going against his parents and being completely selfish.

- The first step which led to his return was when he became aware of his selfishness and the way he had treated his father (verses 18–19).

- The father was already waiting for his son, longing for him to come back home. He ran out to meet his son.

- Instead of punishing his son the father showed love and forgiveness. The only thing necessary was for the son to recognize where he had gone wrong and to be sorry. He even has a party to welcome him home.

What the story teaches

- The relationship between God and people had broken down. People had rebelled against God. They had run away from God in order to follow their own wishes.

- God longs to welcome people back.

In the Bible Paul says that 'God was making mankind his friends through Christ' (2 Corinthians 5:19). Christians believe that Jesus was sent by God to mend the relationship between God and people. Jesus' work of mending that friendship is closely linked with the cross.

Brain Engage

1 Search through a newspaper and identify stories where a relationship has broken down. Who is involved? Name the individuals or groups in each case. What caused the breakdown in each case?

2a The younger son would have been frightened he would be punished. How do you react to the story of the runaway son? Was the father too soft? Why do you think the father did not punish him? Can punishment be part of forgiveness?

2b In pairs sit back to back. One person imagines they are the father. The other is either the runaway son or the elder son. Without talking, write a script of what you would say to each other at the moment when the runaway son returns. Pass the script back to each other after you have written your bit. Act this out in class.

3 Design a poster God might put up, calling people back to him—'to bring back the runaway'.

4 Find John 3:16–17. How does this help you to understand the story of the Runaway Son?

Extra

5 Find out about the work of reconciliation at Coventry Cathedral. Write to the Cathedral asking for information about their work mending friendships. The address is: Coventry Cathedral Education Service, 7, Priory Row, Coventry CV1 5ES.

6 Draw your own cartoon strip showing another reason for breakdown in relationships.

Summary

Christians believe that things have gone wrong in this world because people have rebelled against God. The broken relationship has to be mended to put things right again.

Guilty Or Not Guilty?

After only three years' work Jesus was condemned to death for claiming to be the Son of God.

You are invited to be the jury. Split into small groups. Each group should study one argument, either for or against Jesus being the Son of God. You will need Bibles to look up the evidence. After studying the evidence pick a spokesperson to present the case for the prosecution and the case for the defence.

The case against Jesus

'Members of the jury, I intend to prove to you that this man called Jesus is a liar and troublemaker. He claims he is sent by God yet he has collected around him a band of followers who rebel against all forms of authority—both religious and political. Let's look at the evidence.

1 During the last few years he has made the most outrageous claims: 'I came from God ... he sent me' (John 8:42); 'I am the bread of life' (John 6:35). He goes around forgiving people's sins—acting like God (Mark 2:1–12). Are these really the words of a sane man? No, of course not. They are the rantings of a lunatic. Even at the beginning of his work people clearly saw that he was a madman (Mark 3:21). He has even claimed that God personally called him when he was baptized by John (Mark 1:9–11). It goes without saying that no one else saw or heard anything!

2 He has gone out of his way to disobey the commandments of God. He even claims that God has given him permission to do so. What cheek! Look at the evidence for yourself:

- Instead of obeying the traditional law not to work on the Sabbath Jesus has made a point of working. He tried to heal people on the Sabbath (Luke 4:31–37, 38–39: Luke 14:1–6). He even picked his own food on the Sabbath (Mark 2:23–28).

3 He mixes with all the wrong people—lepers, prostitutes (Luke 7:36–50) and known swindlers—and goes out of his way to insult religious leaders (Matthew 23).

4 He encourages people to behave in ways which are clearly ludicrous. Listen to some of the things he has said:

- "Do not judge others" (Matthew 7:1). Whenever someone wrongs you forgive them, no matter what they have done (Matthew 18:21–35). Such mad talk undermines all sense of right and wrong.

- "If anyone slaps you on the right cheek, let him slap your left cheek too" (Matthew 5:39). He encourages people to take advantage.

- He even goes around telling people not to pay their taxes to the government (Luke 23:2).

Members of the jury, this man has claimed to be a king, the Messiah (Luke 23:2). We all know that the Jews expect the Messiah to overthrow the government and set up his own kingdom. This man is clearly a troublemaker. We must get rid of him before he causes any more harm. I rest my case.'

The case for Jesus

'The case for the prosecution rests on the belief that Jesus was a liar and madman who went around claiming to have powers which he hadn't got. His claims to be the Son of God really are the words of a madman or a villain, unless they are true. Members of the jury, I will prove to you that this man really is the Son of God.

1 The claims he made about himself are true. If he came from God, we would expect him to have God's power. This is exactly what we find when we look at the evidence:

- People have been amazed by the way he speaks (Mark 1:22).

- He can do the most incredible things:

  He has demonstrated his control over nature (Mark 4:37–41).

  He has healed many people (Mark 1:40–42; 2:1–12; 8:22–26).

  He has even brought people back from the dead (Mark 5:22–43; Luke 7:11–15; John 11:1–44). Crowds of people saw him do these things. If he didn't get these powers from God, how do you explain them?

2 He has actually encouraged people to obey God. Jesus has told people to accept God as their king and ruler (Mark 1:14–15). He has told many stories (parables) to illustrate what this means in everyday life.

3 He has mixed with outcasts because he wanted to show them God's love (Mark 10:46–52), not because he was a criminal.

- He respects the Jewish law (Matthew 5:17).

- The only reason the prosecutor and his friends think he is a troublemaker is because he is brave enough to tell the leaders of this country when they fail to obey the law themselves (Matthew 23:3).

4 He hasn't encouraged people to do wrong. What he has said is that none of us is perfect and therefore we should take great care before we judge others (John 8:1–11). He's commanded his followers to be peacemakers, to go out of their way to solve conflict (Matthew 5:9). Yes, Jesus' teaching is revolutionary but not in the way the prosecutor would like you to believe. When he said that he has come to fulfil the law he taught not only that people should do the right thing but they should also feel and think the right thing. Look at the evidence for yourself (Matthew 5: 21–48).

Members of the jury, you have three possible verdicts.

1. Jesus is mad. But his teaching is not that of a madman: it is about love, faith in God and forgiveness.

2. Jesus is bad—a troublemaker. The evidence does not suggest this. He has gone around healing people and teaching them how to do what God wants.

3. Jesus is the Son of God. I believe that this is the only true verdict you can come to.'

The verdict

Find out for yourself what happened at the original trial by tracing the events which led up to Jesus' death:

- **Betrayal by a friend: Matthew 26:47–56**

- **The trials: Mark 14:53–65; Mark 15:1–15**

Brain Engage

1 What crimes was Jesus accused of?

2 Do you think he committed these crimes? Explain your answer.

3 If you were in the jury, how would you vote? Take a class vote.

Summary

Christians believe that Jesus' life and teaching presents people with a challenge, to accept or reject him.

The Suffering God

Do you wear an instrument of torture as a piece of jewellery? You may think it is an odd question—but you would be surprised how many people do.

Look at the picture. Write down all the words and phrases that come to mind to describe what's happening

Jewellery of death

Like the man in the photograph, many people wear crosses around their necks. We think of this as a normal piece of jewellery, but it's really like wearing an electric chair around your neck, or even a syringe full of cyanide!

The South American sculptor, Guido Rocha, was a political prisoner in both Brazil and Chile. In this image of Jesus on the cross he has attempted to use his own experiences to create a sculpture of suffering and pain. He wanted to reflect the suffering of his people in South America in the face of Jesus.

Brain Engage

1 Carry out a survey in your school to find out how many people wear the cross as jewellery. Collect the reasons why they wear it. How many said they wear it as a symbol of their faith?

2 The account of Jesus' crucifixion can be found in all four Gospels. Read Matthew 27:32–56 and Luke 23:26–43. How do they differ? List the suffering Jesus went through, for example beating.

3 The cross is a symbol of a suffering man—weak, helpless, broken. What does this tell you about the Christian view of God?

Death by crucifixion

Crucifixion is a brutal form of execution. Even today people are killed by this vicious method. Jesus died by the Roman method of crucifixion.

● The victim was stripped and whipped. Pieces of bone or iron tore the back open.

● The condemned man had to carry his own heavy cross-beam.

● The hands were nailed to the cross-piece. The feet were tied to the base of the beam and a nail driven through them.

● The body was arranged in such a way that the prisoner could neither ease the pain nor quicken his end.

● It could take many days to die. A Roman soldier plunged his spear into Jesus' side to make sure he was dead.

The Christian symbol

The cross, representing the death of Jesus, is the central symbol of Christianity. But why is the cross so important? Why do Christians choose to remember Jesus with such a terrible symbol?

One reason is that the cross shows what God is like—he is a suffering God. He understands human suffering from the inside. For those who are themselves suffering, this can be a lifeline, helping them to find purpose in suffering.

66 Because Jesus has gone through the worst of agonies I know he understands my suffering. I no longer feel alone. **99**

66 He suffered as a person. That makes you feel better . . . 'cos you know that he's been tempted. He knows what the friction in life is, and the ups and the downs, and to be deserted and lonely. He must have been lonely millions of times. **99**

On the cross God says, 'Not only do I know about your suffering. I have shared in it.'

Brain Engage

4 Make your own collage of the crucifixion. You only need some newspapers and/or colour supplements. Tear up pieces of the newspaper to form your own picture. Do not use scissors. Use glue to stick down your collage.

5 Read Matthew 27:46. Why do you think Jesus felt that God had forsaken him?

Extra

6 Read Matthew 27:32. Imagine you were Simon who carried Jesus' cross. Using both Matthew's and Luke's account of the crucifixion write about the event from his point of view. Show how he might have felt about his involvement.

7 Write about a happy or sad experience in your life which you think you could use to help others, or which helps you to understand others in a similar situation.

Summary

The cross shows that God understands what it is to suffer. Christians believe that 'For our sake he was crucified under Pontius Pilate; he suffered death and was buried' (Apostles' Creed).

The Big Ransom Demand

Hijack in a French Classroom

Shortly after 9.30 a.m. last Thursday morning Eric Schmitt, 42, walked calmly into classroom number eight at a primary school in Paris. For 46 hours he held six infants and their teacher hostage.

Schmitt had told the police in a letter that he had tied a bomb to his waist and had boobytrapped the classroom. He signed the letter HB— 'human bomb'. By lunchtime he had issued his ransom demand. In exchange for the lives of the 21 children in the class he wanted 100 million francs. During the course of the first day and night Schmitt released 15 of his captives. He also demanded a getaway car of the police. His threats were chilling: 'To avoid the fate of a hostage-taker of children, I will not allow myself to be taken alive, and I am determined to blow everything up if I fail.'

More bizarrely, he said he would slowly drain the blood from children if his instructions were not followed. Eric threatened to use the infants as 'human shields' to guarantee his freedom.

The hostage ordeal reached a brutal climax at

Complete the sentence:
A hostage is ....
A ransom is ...

7.25 a.m. today when a specialist team of hooded marksmen smashed into the classroom. Eric was asleep. They carried guns fitted with silencers so as not to frighten the children.

As the hostage-taker struggled to wake up, police marksmen shot him three

times in the head. His six hostages, all girls aged between two-and-a-half and four, were swept straight into the arms of their exhausted parents, who had spent two gruelling nights waiting in a nearby classroom.

A human ransom

On 20 January 1987 Terry Waite, envoy for the Archbishop of Canterbury, disappeared. He had come to Lebanon to seek the release of more than twenty Westerners who were held hostage. Instead, he himself was taken hostage and held for four long years in Beirut. He had known the danger of his task. He was willing to risk his own freedom—and possibly his life—in order to secure the release of others. He became a living ransom, spending 1,763 days alone in a darkened cell.

In an interview on BBC1 shortly after his release he described what he had to endure as a hostage.

❝ I was kept in an underground cell. I was totally blindfolded, chained hand and foot so that I couldn't lie straight and I couldn't stand up. People would come in the early hours of the morning. They'd unchain my hands and say, 'Face the wall.' Then someone would throw questions at me from behind. It went on like that perhaps for a couple of hours, sometimes accompanied by physical violence. **❞**

The photograph shows Terry Waite and bodyguard in Beirut, shortly before he was taken hostage.

Mission accomplished

These two stories give us an idea of what being a hostage is like. People take hostages because they want something. So hostages suffer and lose their freedom.

The first Christians used the idea of ransom to help show the meaning of Jesus' death. His life was seen as the payment made by God himself to secure the freedom of people who are hostages to sin and death.

At the moment of his death Jesus cried out: 'It is finished.' By this he meant that the ransom is paid. Jesus paid with his life for all the wrong thoughts, words and actions of all the people who have ever lived.

Christians believe that because of his death they can be free. They believe that Jesus has made it possible for everyone who trusts him to have a fresh start.

Dying For Others

Bridge on the River Kwai

Christians believe that Jesus died for other people. They have tried to explain this in many ways. Here we look at two of these ideas: that Jesus was a substitute (that he took the place of others) and that he was a bridge linking God and humanity.

This story, about some British soldiers of the Argyll Regiment who were captured by the Japanese, is taken from Ernest Gordon's book *Miracle on the River Kwai*.

The day's work had ended; the tools were being counted as usual. As the work party was about to be dismissed, the Japanese guard shouted that a shovel was missing. He insisted that someone had stolen it to sell it. Striding up and down before the men, he ranted and denounced them for their wickedness and, most unforgivable of all, their ingratitude to the Emperor. Screaming in broken English, he demanded that the guilty one step forward to take his punishment. No one moved; the guard's rage reached new heights of violence. 'All die! All die!' he shrieked.

To show that he meant what he said, he put his rifle to his shoulder and aimed ready to fire at the first man at the end of the line. At that moment a soldier stepped forward, stood stiffly to attention and said calmly, 'I did it.' The guard unleashed all his fury; he kicked the helpless prisoner and beat him with his fists. Still the soldier stood rigidly to attention, with the blood streaming down his face. His silence made the guard more furious. Seizing his rifle by the barrel, he lifted it high over his head and, with a final blow, brought it down on the skull of the soldier, who sank limply to the ground and did not move. Although it was perfectly clear that he was dead the guard continued to beat him and stopped only when exhausted.

The men of the work detail picked up their friend's body, shouldered their tools and marched back to camp. When the tools were counted again at the guard house no shovel was missing. That Argyll soldier died on behalf of others. Christians believe that Jesus also died on behalf of others. Both were innocent: they did not deserve to die. But, if they had not died, others would have done.

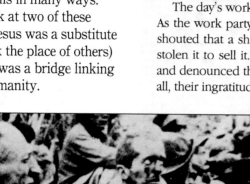

Bring on the substitute

When have you heard that before? A substitute is somebody who takes another person's place. There are some remarkable stories in history of people who have 'stood in', become substitutes for others who were about to die. The River Kwai story took place in the Second World War.

Christians find that the idea of substitution helps them understand the crucifixion. The Bible says that everyone has sinned and is far away from God. The penalty for sin is death. But Jesus died instead, not for good people but for bad ones. Christians believe that this demonstrates how great God's love is for every human being.

Bridging the gap

One of the worst sea accidents in recent years happened on 6 March 1987. The ferry, *Herald of Free Enterprise*, capsized outside Zeebrugge harbour killing many people. Doors in the car deck had been accidentally left open, and water flooded in.

In the middle of this tragedy one man stands out as a hero. He was Andrew Parker. He saw two metal barriers above his head. He stretched between them and made himself a human bridge. People were then able to climb up his body to safety. Twenty people were saved this way.

Catherine of Siena (1347–80) described Jesus as a bridge. A bridge joins people and places that are separated. Christians believe that on the cross Jesus bridged the gap between God who is altogether good, loving and just, and sinful human beings. Jesus' death put things right: God's enemies could now be his friends.

Christians call this belief the *atonement* (at-one-ment). Jesus bridged the gap and made it possible for people to be 'at one' with God.

Summary

Christians believe that Jesus died as a substitute on people's behalf. By his death he bridged the gap between people and God and brought them back together again. This belief is called the *atonement*.

Brain Engage

1 Can you imagine ever being willing to take the blame and punishment for something you didn't do? Write a story in which someone does this.

2 If you had been one of the Argyll Regiment what would you do to remember this brave act each year? Design a symbol you would wear to commemorate it.

3 The Roman governor, Pilate, wanted to set Jesus free, but the crowd asked for Barabbas (a murderer) to be freed instead. Read his story in Mark 15:6–15. Write the entry for Barabbas' diary the day after he was set free. Describe what happened and try to describe the feelings Barabbas may have had.

4 A man's life is a lot to pay! Did Jesus have to die? Wasn't there an easier way? What answers would a Christian give to these questions? Write a conversation between two people discussing these questions. Look up John 3:16–17. What does that say about the reason for Jesus' death?

5 Read Romans 5:6–8. Build up a picture display with this verse as the central feature.

Remember, Remember . . .

Anniversaries, centenaries: we have all kinds of ways of keeping important past events fresh in our memories. Sometimes a whole town or country remembers an event in a special way. By calling an event to mind, people go back into the past and enter into it.

Remembering the fans who died: 200,000 people filed through the Anfield stadium, leaving a carpet of scarves and flowers.

Tragedy at FA Cup Semi-final – 94 trapped and crushed

In April 1989 94 people died and 169 were injured at Hillsborough as they watched the FA Cup semi-final game between Liverpool and Nottingham Forest. Moments after the match had begun thousands of extra Liverpool fans were allowed into the Hillsborough ground. People near the barriers were squashed to death as helpless spectators looked on.

Within days the people of Liverpool found a way of remembering their dead. They collected football scarves of the two Merseyside teams and tied them together to make a continuous link between the two grounds. In addition, the pitch at Liverpool's ground was carpeted with flowers and scarves. Both symbolic gestures were aimed at keeping the memory of the dead alive. Throughout the following weeks many fans came to the ground. They came to be quiet and to think. They left behind many objects which were precious to them. They brought them as a way of showing their sadness.

'Do this in memory of me'

The night before his death on the cross Jesus ate a meal with his disciples. Christians call this the Last Supper. During the meal Jesus told his disciples that they were to remember him in a special way.

2,000 years on . . .

Nearly 2,000 years later, each day Jesus' command is carried out in churches throughout the world. By eating the bread and drinking the wine Christians are calling to mind Jesus' death on the cross. They break the bread to remember the breaking of his body. They pour the wine to remember his blood being spilt. As they eat and drink they remember what Jesus has done for them by dying. They also believe that Jesus is present in a very special way whenever they celebrate this meal together.

66 When the priest breaks the loaf and pours the wine it's as if the meal in the Upper Room was happening now and Jesus is telling us how much he loves us, enough to die for us. **99**

66 In communion I take the bread as a symbol of God giving strength to me. It strengthens me for all the things I have to do during the week. **99**

66 When I'm actually eating the bread and drinking the wine I usually think about what Jesus has done for me. Jesus died for me. I know he died for everybody else as well. But that's very personal. It also links me with all the other Christians. **99**

66 When I take the communion cup of wine I am reminded that the blood of Jesus constantly forgives my sin. **99**

66 *[Jesus took his place at the table with the apostles.] While they were eating, Jesus took a piece of bread, gave a prayer of thanks, broke the bread, and gave it to his disciples.*

'Take it,' he said, 'this is my body, which is given for you. Do this in memory of me.'

Then he took a cup, gave thanks to God, and handed it to them; and they all drank from it.

Jesus said, 'This is my blood which is poured out for many, my blood which seals God's covenant' **99**

MARK 14:22–26; LUKE 22:14–23

Brain Engage

1a Think back over your life. Which events stand out in your memory? Why are they important?

1b What are you celebrating on your birthday?

2 People like to remember loved ones who have died. How do they do this?

3 The Last Supper is regularly celebrated in churches. Write a set of questions you might ask
(a) the vicar/priest/minister
(b) the Christian after the service about what happens and what it means.

4 Draw the symbols of bread and wine. Write a sentence on each to indicate their meaning for Christians.

Summary

Christians remember the importance of the death of Jesus by celebrating his last supper with the disciples.

The Day Death Died

An amazing surprise

According to the Bible, Jesus' body was taken down from the cross before sunset on the Friday he died. By the Sunday it had vanished. One of his followers, a woman called Mary Magdalene, was the first to see Jesus alive again. Jesus' return from the dead is called the *resurrection*.

This is how John, one of the Gospel writers, describes what happened:

66 Mary stood crying outside the tomb. While she was still crying, she bent over and looked in the tomb and saw two angels, dressed in white, sitting where the body of Jesus had been ... 'Woman, why are you crying?' they asked her. She answered, 'They have taken my Lord away, and I do not know where they have put him!' Then she turned round and saw Jesus standing there; but she did not know that it was Jesus. 'Woman, why are you crying?' Jesus asked her. 'Who is it that you are looking for?' She thought he was the gardener, so she said to him, 'If you took him away, sir, tell me where you have put him, and I will go and get him.' Jesus said to her, 'Mary!' She turned towards him and said in Hebrew, 'Rabboni!' (This means 'Teacher'.) 'Do not hold on to me,' Jesus told her, 'because I have not yet gone back up to the Father.' 99

JOHN 20:11–17

Easter is celebrated all over the world by the lighting of candles to show the passing of Jesus from the darkness of the tomb to the light of new life. In the Orthodox church in Russia the priest approaches the main door of the church with the words of Mary: 'They have taken my Lord away.' The congregation reply with the angel's words, 'He is not here, he is risen.' At that point the flame of the priest's candle is used to light the other worshippers candles. The light of Jesus' resurrection fills the church.

Piecing the evidence together

The empty tomb

Matthew 27:62–66; Mark 16:1–8; Luke 24:1–12; John 20:1–10.

Resurrection appearances

Matthew 28:1–15; Mark 16:9–18; Luke 24:13–49; John 20:11–29; 1 Corinthians 15:3–7.

Aslan's Death

The Chronicles of Narnia, stories by C.S. Lewis, explore the meaning of Christian beliefs. They begin when some children are playing hide-and-seek in a country house. Pushing through a wardrobe full of fur coats they discover the secret land of Narnia which is ruled by a wicked Witch as its Queen. All the creatures of Narnia live in fear of the Queen. When she captures one of the boys, only Aslan the lion can help. He agrees to be a sacrifice instead of the captured boy, is tied to a stone table and killed by the Witch's knife.

That night as two of the children keep watch over the stone altar on which Aslan has been killed they hear a cracking noise behind them:

The rising of the sun had made everything look so different—all colours and shadows were changed—that for a moment they didn't see the important thing. Then they did. The Stone Table was broken into two pieces by a great crack that ran down it from end to end; and there was no Aslan.

'Who's done it?' cried Susan. 'What does it mean? Is it magic?'

'Yes!' said a great voice behind their backs. 'It is more magic.' They looked round. There, shining in the sunrise, larger than they had seen him before, shaking his mane, stood Aslan himself.

'Oh, Aslan!' cried both the children, staring up at him, almost as much frightened as they were glad.

'Aren't you dead then, dear Aslan?' said Lucy.

'Not now,' said Aslan.

'Oh, you're real, you're real! Oh, Aslan!' cried Lucy, and both girls flung themselves upon him and covered him with kisses.

'But what does it all mean?' asked Susan when they were somewhat calmer.

'It means,' said Aslan, 'that though the Witch knew the Deep Magic, there is a magic deeper still which she did not know. Her knowledge goes back only to the dawn of time. But if she could have looked a little further back, into the stillness and the darkness before Time dawned, she would have read there a different incantation. She would have known that when a willing victim who had committed no treachery was killed in a traitor's stead, the Table would crack and Death itself would start working backwards.'

C.S.LEWIS, *THE LION, THE WITCH AND THE WARDROBE*

Lewis, a Christian, is exploring the belief that Jesus' resurrection was a victory, not a defeat. Writing 'death itself would start working backwards' is a good way of expressing the idea of life breaking the power of death. Christians believe not only that Jesus was raised from death, but that for all who trust him there is new life now which cannot end.

Brain Engage

1 Carry out a survey amongst your class to find out what people think happens after death. Write down what your own views are.

2 Write your own poem or short story using the following sentence as your last words: 'Death itself would start working backwards.'

3 In groups, find out if anyone has been in a situation when the presence of light has changed things—for example, being lost in the dark; being ill or worried at night.

4 Design a symbol for Jesus' resurrection. Explain your choice.

5 Although resurrection is a belief about what happens when we die, there are many 'little resurrections' happening all around us—something given new life. Try completing the sentence, 'Resurrection is . . .' You can use pictures from magazines to illustrate the things you say about resurrection.

Summary

Christians believe that Jesus rose from the dead: 'On the third day he rose again' (Apostles' Creed)

Easter Without Chocolate

Easter is so important to Christians that they celebrate it in many different ways.

Oberammergau

In 1633 the Austrian village of Oberammergau was a terrifying place to visit. The smell of the Black Death hung in the air and every day people were dying. Eighty-four people had already died when the villagers met in the church. A decision was taken to make a bargain with God. They promised that they would act out a Passion Play—a play about Jesus' life and death—every ten years if God would save them from the plague. The records from the time show that no further deaths occurred in Oberammergau. The villagers have kept their promise ever since.

The play is a very big tourist attraction. It is acted out as realistically as possible—men are expected to grow beards for the performance, and real animals are used. Each performance lasts for eight hours and involves 700 actors:

❝ As we act out the events of Jesus' life and death we start to understand the pain and cost of what Jesus did. ❞

❝ By retelling the story we discover the meaning of the death of Jesus. God saved our ancestors from the Black Death in 1633. We re-enact this play to show that Jesus came to save not just our village but all people. ❞

What makes fireworks so exciting? They have that spark to fill a dark sky with a mass of multi-coloured light.

In some countries, at midnight on Easter Eve, Christians celebrate the resurrection of Jesus by setting off fireworks.

The story of Jesus' death is so central to Christianity that it is re-enacted in many other places each Easter. All over the world Good Friday is a serious day when Christians identify with the suffering of Jesus. In the Philippines people actually go through part of the crucifixion itself.

An extraordinary re-enactment of Jesus Christ's crucifixion in observance of Holy Week in the Philippines. When the person in the role of Jesus on the cross has lost consciousness they are taken down and looked after until they are well.

'By following in Jesus' footsteps we are attempting to understand what his suffering meant—to understand the pain he went through for us.'

For Christians every Sunday is a celebration of Easter Day. It was because Jesus rose from the dead on a Sunday that the first Jewish Christians changed their day of rest from a Saturday to a Sunday. Russian Christians call Sunday *Voskresnie* ('Resurrection Day').

Easter fire

Many years ago, Saint Patrick, the patron saint of Ireland, lit a bonfire to show the new life which God brought into the world when he raised Jesus from the dead. It happened soon after he had arrived in Ireland to convert the country to Christianity. A pagan festival fell on the night before Easter. The custom of the people was to put out all their fires until the land was utterly dark.

However, instead of keeping this custom Patrick, with other Christians travelling with him, climbed the hill across from the local chief's home. There he lit the great Easter fire. The local priests, called druids, commanded that it be destroyed so the chieftain sent warriors. But no matter how much water and sand they used, the Easter fire kept burning. This was the turning-point for Patrick's work in Ireland. From then on many people believed in Patrick's message.

Pope John Paul II called Christians 'Easter people' because they believe that they can be changed by the God who raised Jesus from the dead and defeated death itself.

Easter eggs

Why do people give eggs to each other at Easter?

From the outside a bird's egg looks dead—it is like the stone which was rolled in front of Jesus' grave. However, inside the egg there is life.

In Orthodox churches boiled eggs are dyed bright red to remind people of Jesus' death. On Easter morning the eggs are cracked against each other (like in a game of conkers). When an egg cracks it reminds people of Jesus breaking out of the tomb.

The contrast between the sadness of Good Friday and the happiness of Easter Sunday is reflected in the way churches are decorated. In some churches all decoration is removed on Good Friday. In other churches all decorations are covered in dark cloth. On Easter Sunday churches are decorated with flowers.

Brain Engage

1 Describe the scene at Oberammergau just before the villagers made their bargain with God. Concentrate on looking at their feelings and what they were asking of God.

2 Design a brochure advertising the Oberammergau play. Say something about its meaning.

3 Look at the pictures. Make a list of words and phrases that express the feelings of Easter.

4 Using the information on this page make up some designs to go on Easter eggs which would help people buying them understand the importance of Easter for Christians.

Extra

5 Write an argument between two characters—one called Life and one called Death—as to which is the stronger. Act it out as a play.

Summary

Christians celebrate the death and resurrection of Jesus at Easter time every year. Countries around the world have their own customs based on the meaning of the Easter events.

A New Beginning

Mission Complete

Forty days after Easter, Christians celebrate 'Ascension Day'. They remember the time when Jesus, having completed the mission he had come to do on earth, returned to his Father in heaven. The risen Jesus had been with his disciples for forty days when 'he was taken up to heaven as they watched him, and a cloud hid him from their sight.'

Luke goes on to record that

66 They still had their eyes fixed on the sky as he went away, when two men dressed in white suddenly stood beside them and said, 'Galileans, why are you standing there looking up at the sky? This Jesus, who was taken from you into heaven, will come back in the same way that you saw him go to heaven.' 99

ACTS 1:10–11

Imagine that you were on the first Apollo space mission to the moon. Write your diary entry on the day you return, including your feelings about: having completed your mission; what you have achieved; what it is like to be safely back home.

▲ The first men to walk the moon returned home to a great reception.

What does it mean to call someone your king? What would you be willing to do for a king?

Just as the Apollo explorers returned home to receive garlands of honour so the church pictures Jesus ruling as King over the universe. Some paintings of Jesus do not leave him on the cross, as in this picture, but show him with a crown on his head, for he is king. Jesus rules with outstretched arms that have been pierced by nails.

 DID YOU KNOW? When Luke says that Jesus 'was taken up to heaven … and a cloud hid him' he did not necessarily mean this to be taken literally, any more than 'moving up' in school means going to the top floor of the school building. 'Going up to heaven' means that Jesus was returning to a better state—'higher', to be with God his Father. The Bible often uses the idea of a cloud to describe God's presence.

Brain Engage

1 What promise was given to Jesus' disciples by the angels when they saw him taken up into heaven?

> *If some kids say that the church is boring I would say that they're wrong. It's exciting. The Bible says, 'make a joyful sound to the Lord'.*

Pentecost

Before his death Jesus told his disciples that it would be necessary for him to go away in order that the Holy Spirit might come to be their helper (John 15:26; 16:7). The Holy Spirit is also described as the 'Spirit of God' or the 'Spirit of Jesus'.

On the fiftieth day after Easter, at Pentecost (the Greek name for the Jewish festival of wheat harvest), Jesus' followers were all together in Jerusalem.

66 Suddenly there was a noise from the sky which sounded like a strong wind blowing, and it filled the whole house where they were sitting. Then they saw what looked like tongues of fire which spread out and touched each person there. They were all filled with the Holy Spirit and began to talk in other languages, as the Spirit enabled them to speak. 99

ACTS 2:1–4

When the apostles received the Holy Spirit they were changed people. Instead of being frightened followers who were in hiding in Jerusalem they became courageous. They went out to preach the good news, facing danger and even death. God was with them in a new way, giving them strength and guidance and the power to heal as Jesus had done. The history of the first Christians—the early church—is told in The Acts of the Apostles. This book of the Bible could just as well be called 'The Acts of the Holy Spirit' because it is the story of how the Holy Spirit guides and strengthens the followers of Jesus.

Summary

'On the third day Jesus rose again . . . he ascended into heaven . . . We believe in the Holy Spirit, who proceeds from the Father and the Son' (Apostles' Creed).

The Pentecostal Church

The name for a large branch of the Christian church today comes from the feast of Pentecost when Christians celebrate the coming of the Holy Spirit to the apostles. Pentecostal Christians put particular stress on the work of the Holy Spirit in teaching, guiding and enabling Christians to witness to their faith; and on special gifts God's Spirit gives to the church today as he did in New Testament times. Their worship is often lively—with dancing and clapping.

The Pentecostal movement began in the United States in 1906 and spread rapidly. Today there are about 410 million Pentecostal Christians. In Britain they are especially strong in the black community. The movement combines free and joyful worship with strict Bible-based beliefs. 'Charismatic' is another word for Pentecostal. It comes from a Greek word meaning 'gift' and relates to the gifts of the Spirit mentioned by Paul (1 Corinthians 12:1–11).

Brain Engage

2 Make a list of the qualities of wind (for example: gentle, cooling). What can it do?

3 With a partner imagine that you were there at the time of Pentecost. One of you is to be an interviewer, the other a member of those gathered in the room. Conduct a conversation about what happened and how this experience changed people.

The Holy Spirit in the Church

On the day of Pentecost, the Holy Spirit came to the disciples. To those who saw it, it seemed as though tongues of fire fell on them and there was a sound like a strong wind. Fire and wind are frequent Bible pictures of the Holy Spirit, expressing God's holiness purifying his people.

At Pentecost the disciples felt full of a new power—the power of the Holy Spirit—which gave them fresh courage, confidence and abilities they'd never had before. Christians believe that this power is still available and at work in the world today.

Water pours over the Victoria Falls: it provides a picture of the Holy Spirit, clean and life-giving.

Symbols for the Holy Spirit

The Holy Spirit is God's living presence with people. This cannot be seen, so a number of images are used to describe it:

● Wind

A noise like a rushing wind occurs in the story in Acts 2. You cannot see the wind but you can see the results of its power. Similarly you can see the power of the Holy Spirit in people's lives, changing them, but you cannot actually see the Holy Spirit.

The power of the wind makes these kites fly: the power of the Holy Spirit, like the wind, is real though it cannot be seen.

● Water

The Holy Spirit is likened to 'living' water. Water gives life and water cleanses and refreshes. The cleansing links the Holy Spirit with baptism. God said, 'I will give water to the thirsty land ... I will pour out my power on your children ... They will thrive like well watered grass.'

● Fire

The Holy Spirit burns away things which are wrong, and makes people's lives beautiful.

● Breath

The word used for 'spirit' in the Bible means 'breath'. God gave Adam the breath of life and he became a living being. In the story of Ezekiel (Ezekiel 37:1–14) the dry bones he saw came together but they did not live until breath entered them. The Holy Spirit is the life-giving Spirit.

● Dove

The dove is a symbol of peace. The Holy Spirit was seen as a dove at Jesus' baptism. This is the gentler side of the Spirit: bringing peace, unity and reconciliation.

What does the Holy Spirit do?

66 The Holy Spirit helps me to keep God's commandments. 99

LINDA, 19

66 Without the Holy Spirit I wouldn't have a clue how to pray. 99

MIKE, 17

66 When I am feeling down I sometimes feel the Holy Spirit touch me with God's love and hope. 99

JO, 14

66 The Holy Spirit helps me to understand what I read in the Bible. It brings it to life for me and makes it relevant to my life. 99

ANNIE, 14

Sometimes, as the newspaper reports, the Holy Spirit works in dramatic ways.

Holy Spirit Hits London

The work of the Holy Spirit has been seen dramatically in churches across the world. It all appears to have begun at the Airport Vineyard church in Toronto, Canada in August 1994. The Holy Spirit has come with such power upon prayer meetings, church services and even staff business meetings that people are talking in terms of a revival.

Charismatic phenomena, listed by Paul in Corinthians, include healing, prophecy and speaking in tongues. The Sunday services during the last two weeks have resulted in scores of people lying all over the floor, with prayers continuing for many hours afterwards. Those affected speak of how they have been given a renewed sense of God's love for them, and a new joy to serve him. This is happening in churches all over London.

'When I arrived at the evening service I was feeling very frustrated and filled with anger to do with work. When Sandy started praying for everyone to be filled with the Spirit I felt my arms starting to move. I felt all the anger go and after that I felt the Spirit was on me for the whole of the rest of the evening. I feel closer to God.'

How do you know if someone is a Christian? Saint Paul was quite clear in his answer to this question. When a person becomes a Christian you will be able to see the 'fruit of the Spirit' at work in their life. He went on to show the marks of God working in someone's life:

66 The Spirit produces love, joy, peace, patience, kindness, goodness, faithfulness, humility and self-control. 99

GALATIANS 5:22–23

Christians know that it is a lifelong task to develop these qualities; it doesn't just happen overnight.

66 Just because I am trying to live as God wants me to live doesn't make it all easy. Sometimes it is an uphill struggle, since my human nature still has other desires. 99

JUSTIN, 17

Brain Engage

1 Design a banner to show how the Holy Spirit works in someone's life. Use as many of the symbols of the Holy Spirit as you can.

2 Use this page to make a list of reasons Christians give for believing in the Holy Spirit.

3 Draw your own 'Tree of the Spirit' for the classroom. On it hang the fruits of the Spirit.

4 Write a paragraph explaining what you understand Christians mean when they talk about the Holy Spirit.

Summary

'We believe in the Holy Spirit, the Lord, the giver of life' (Apostles' Creed).

Power to Change

When a person becomes a Christian he or she begins a new life. With the help of the Holy Spirit a self-centred life begins to change to a God-centred one.

Sometimes the effect the Holy Spirit has on people's lives is very sudden and dramatic. Jackie Pullinger has witnessed many of these changes in her work in Hong Kong's former Walled City.

This was a no-go area where strangers were unwelcome and police hesitated to enter. It was a haven for drug smuggling and illegal gambling. Prostitution, pornography and heroin addiction flourished. 30,000 people—maybe twice that—lived in a few cramped acres.

When Jackie Pullinger set out for Hong Kong from England she had no idea that God was calling her to work in the Walled City. Yet, as she spoke to them of Jesus, brutal Triad gangsters were converted, prostitutes quit, and Jackie discovered a new 'treatment' for drug addiction: the power of the Holy Spirit in the lives of new Christians. Over the last twenty years Jackie has seen countless lives changed as addicts, often close to death, have been given a new lease of life by God.

Stephen, Jonathan and Luke (just three of many) tell their own stories of how they were changed by the work of the Holy Spirit in their lives:

> ❝ I walked in one night and was amazed. I saw ones I'd been to school with, to prison with, with whom I'd chased the dragon, others whom I'd fought. Each one had changed, and as I talked with them, they were so different. ❞
>
> STEPHEN

Luke came off drugs after seventeen years of addiction:

> ❝ I was told that with Jackie there was no medication to come off drugs, only prayer. I did not know how this could work, but some of the people who prayed with me—and whom I had known when they were addicts—told me it was true, so I believed them. So I prayed: 'Jesus, I confess my sin and ask you into my life and ask you to heal me. Amen.' It was wonderful. When I said 'Amen', all the pain stopped. I felt very comfortable and peaceful. I fell asleep; usually I could never sleep when trying to come off drugs. ❞

Jonathan joined a gang when he was fourteen. He spent much of his youth in and out of boys' homes and detention centres. When he first became an addict his parents tried everything to get him off drugs—from locking him in the house to sending him to a government treatment centre in China.

> ❝ Then Jackie came to the centre. That was when I first heard of her home and of Jesus. When I returned to Hong Kong I was back on heroin, I was fed up with my life. I met up with Jackie. Getting off drugs was surprisingly painless, through praying. But it was the care and concern which overwhelmed me—it was the first time in my life that I felt really loved. I understand now God's faithfulness and his patience. I am changing, now I am slow to anger. I have learned to think, and if something is wrong, even unfair, I can accept it, I can work through it. ❞
>
> JONATHAN

Jackie Pullinger in Hong Kong.

Jesus talked about the need to be changed when he talked to a Jewish leader called Nicodemus. He came to Jesus late one night and said to him, 'Rabbi, we know that you are a teacher sent by God. No one could perform the miracles you are doing unless God were with him.' Jesus answered, 'I am telling you the truth: no one can see the Kingdom of God unless he is born again.' 'How can a grown man be born again?' Nicodemus asked. 'He certainly cannot enter his mother's womb and be born a second time!' 'I am telling you the truth,' replied Jesus. 'No one can enter the Kingdom of God unless he is born of water and the Spirit. A person is born physically of human parents, but he is born spiritually of the Spirit' (John 3:1–6).

Most Christians experience the work of the Holy Spirit in their lives in a less dramatic way than the examples here. What they have in common with Stephen, Luke and Jonathan is that their lives change direction when they receive the Holy Spirit: and the work of inner transformation goes on all through their lives.

Brain Engage

1 Look through each of the accounts and write a 'before' and 'after' for each person.

2 Christians believe that the Holy Spirit helps them understand what God is like and how he works. From reading these case-stories, what might Christians learn about God?

Extra:

3 Spirit is not 'material'—not physical like a body. Many Christians and others talk about the human spirit. What do you think they mean by this?

Summary

Christians believe that the Holy Spirit changes people's lives.

The Maker's Manual

Have you ever been to a maze? It is very easy to get lost in good mazes: people can spend hours trying to find their way out.

Mazes like this one at Breamore are designed to confuse: you can't see the design, except from above.

Perhaps you have taken something to pieces, tried to put it back together again, and found that it doesn't work? Many people buy manuals for their bike so that they can try to do minor jobs. Sometimes they get a bit ambitious!

What do you think the person in the photo below would say if you asked why they read this ancient book?

Life can be as bewildering as a maze or the inside of an engine. We could all do with a manual or a guide for that. Where some people look to heroes or a political party for direction Christians use the Bible as their guide. In the beginning Christians called themselves 'followers of the Way' ('Christians' was a nickname others gave them). Their map through life was the teaching we now have in the Bible. They believed this was God the Maker's manual on how to live.

Christians often call the Bible the 'word of God'. This does not mean that God dictated every sentence, but that the ideas the writers had came from God. This is why many people think that it is so special and that its message speaks to people of every age. It deals with things that do not change: love, anger, forgiveness; with spending money or using the right priorities when it comes to time; with life and death.

66 Whoever made this book made me; it knows all that is in my heart. 99

A CHINESE READER OF THE NEW TESTAMENT

66 When I'm not sure what to do in a situation I turn to the Bible. It is full of advice on how to live and deal with difficult situations. For example, the other day I was so angry with my friend Marek. Before I went to bed I read that bit in the Bible where it says about judging others. It made sense. I guess I hadn't been nice to him. It helped me sort out how I should deal with the situation. 99

IAN, 16

The Bible's message has changed millions of lives and whole countries.

Hercule Poirot solves the mystery of life

David Suchet, the actor who plays the famous TV detective, Hercule Poirot, found that the Bible gave him the best clues he had ever found in his search for the meaning of life.

'While lying in the bath I felt a desperate need to read the Bible. Why? I don't know. (I hadn't read any of it since my schooldays!) In the New Testament I suddenly discovered the way that life should be followed.'

The effect of opening the Bible that day in 1986 has been great. It has changed the way he views his work.

'The problems come when you are given lines or asked to read scripts that are blasphemous, licentious, overtly sensual and things like that,' he explains. David prays about such matters. Whereas previously he would have played the dubious roles, he says now he has the confidence to turn them down.

Some people have risked their lives in order to make the Bible available to others.

William Tyndale (1492–1536) wanted to translate the New Testament from Greek to English so that ordinary people could read it. The Bishop of London refused him permission. In fear of his life he had to escape to Germany to finish the work.

Copies printed in Germany were smuggled into England. King Henry VIII ordered them to be burned.

On 6 October 1536, while Tyndale was working on the Old Testament in Antwerp, he was betrayed, arrested and burned at the stake. 'Lord, open the King of England's eyes,' he prayed.

In 1539 the first complete Bible was printed in England—with King Henry VIII's blessing.

Summary

The Bible is the Christian's guide through life.

Brain Engage

1 How does life appear to you? Is it a maze, is it a journey on a road, a voyage at sea? Draw a picture/symbol of life to reflect how you see it—or write about it.

2 Write a story about someone who buys something, such as a microwave, and ignores the instructions.

3 The Bible is described in a number of ways. Look up the references to see what each is saying. It is described as a mirror (James 1:23); a sword (Ephesians 6:17; Hebrews 4:12); a hammer (Jeremiah 23:29); a fire (Jeremiah 20:9); a lamp or light (Psalm 119: 105); food (Hebrews 5:12—6:1).

4 The Bible gives instructions on how to live. Read Romans 12:9–21.

5 Why do you think people have Bibles but don't read them?

The World's Bestseller

If you go into a bookshop and ask for the world's bestselling book, what will they give you? If they know the book trade well they will hand you a Bible.

In fact the Bible is not one book but a collection of books. The word 'Bible' comes from the Greek word *biblia* meaning books. It is like a small library made up of sixty-six books. It took many people over a thousand years to write. Like any library it is made up of different types of books—law, history, songs, poetry, prophecy, letters, Gospels and much more.

The Bible is divided into two parts: the Old Testament and the New Testament. A testament is a covenant or promise (see pages 12 and 13). By calling the two parts of the Bible Old and New Testaments, Christians are saying that the Bible is the story of God's promises to people and their relationship with him.

The World's Most Used Library

THE BIBLE

Volume 1—called the Hebrew Bible or, by Christians, the Old Testament—is the Jewish holy book.

Most of it was written in Hebrew (the language spoken by Israeli people today).

It contains 39 books (from Genesis to Malachi).

It tells the story of the creation of the world and the beginnings of the Jewish race; of how God chose Abraham to be the 'father of the Jews'. It charts their history: how a nomadic people became the nation of Israel. It is the story of God's love for his 'chosen people'. However, it also tells how people have turned away from his love, and have broken their promises to him (the covenant).

Volume 2—the New Testament—was written in Greek, although it also contains some words of Aramaic, the language Jesus spoke.

It contains 27 books (from Matthew to Revelation).

It has four accounts of Jesus' life: the 'Gospels' (meaning 'good news').

It also tells the history of the first Christians (in the Acts of the Apostles and the letters of Paul and other apostles).

The last book, Revelation, is a collection of visions given (revealed) to John by God.

In the fourth century the Old and New Testaments were translated into Latin. Since the sixteenth century the whole Bible has been translated into some 800 languages, and parts of it are available in over 2,000 languages.

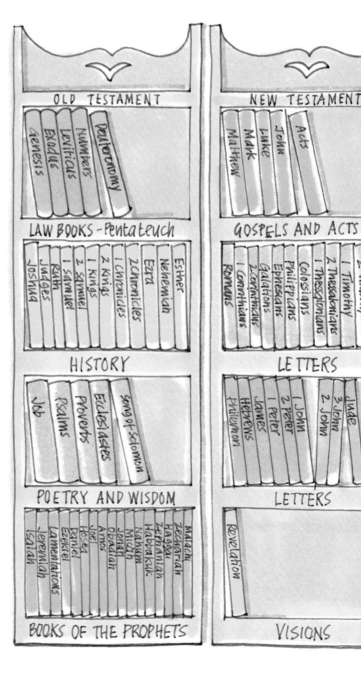

OLD TESTAMENT

LAW BOOKS – Pentateuch
Genesis, Exodus, Leviticus, Numbers, Deuteronomy

HISTORY
Joshua, Judges, Ruth, 1 Samuel, 2 Samuel, 1 Kings, 2 Kings, 1 Chronicles, 2 Chronicles, Ezra, Nehemiah, Esther

POETRY AND WISDOM
Job, Psalms, Proverbs, Ecclesiastes, Song of Solomon

BOOKS OF THE PROPHETS
Isaiah, Jeremiah, Lamentations, Ezekiel, Daniel, Hosea, Joel, Amos, Obadiah, Jonah, Micah, Nahum, Habakkuk, Zephaniah, Haggai, Zechariah, Malachi

NEW TESTAMENT

GOSPELS AND ACTS
Matthew, Mark, Luke, John, Acts

LETTERS
Romans, 1 Corinthians, 2 Corinthians, Galatians, Ephesians, Philippians, Colossians, 1 Thessalonians, 2 Thessalonians, 1 Timothy, 2 Timothy, Titus

LETTERS
Philemon, Hebrews, James, 1 Peter, 2 Peter, 1 John, 2 John, 3 John, Jude

VISIONS
Revelation

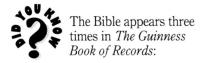
The Bible today

One very important development in Latin America has been the understanding of the Bible from a third-world point of view. It's not just about private religious experience. It's actually engaging with the huge issues of poverty, justice and peace in their community life and the life of their countries.

⚬ Brain Engage

1 Design a book cover for each volume of the Bible.

2 Make a list of the reasons Christians give for saying that the Bible is important.

Summary

Christians believe that the Bible contains God's message to humanity, and that it has the power to change lives.

Power to change

Ernest Gordon (who wrote *Miracle on the River Kwai*) tells of the amazing change that took place in a Japanese prisoner-of-war camp in Burma between Christmas 1942 and Christmas 1943. In 1942 the camp was a sea of mud and filth. It was a scene of sweated labour and brutal treatment by the Japanese guards. There was hardly any food, and everyone looked only after himself. Twelve months later, the ground of the camp was cleared and clean. Huts had been rebuilt and on Christmas morning 2,000 men were at worship. What had happened?

During the year a prisoner had shared his last crumb of food with another man who was also in desperate need. Then he had died. Amongst his belongings they found a Bible. Could this be the secret of his life, of his willingness to give to others and not to grasp for himself? One by one the prisoners began to read it. Soon the Spirit of God began to grip their hearts and change their lives.

Understanding the Book

There are many different types of writing in the Bible: history, poetry, biography... The kind of writing you choose for a particular purpose is important. For example, try the following exercise:

> Choose one of the two pictures. First write a love letter to this person. Then write a description of the person to give to the police as a report of a missing person.

> How do the two pieces of writing differ?

> Which tells you more about the person? Explain your answer.

The Bible uses a number of ways to speak about God—poetry, history, prophecy, prayers, songs, parables and laws ... When reading the Bible an important question to ask is 'What kind of writing is this—what was the writer trying to do when this passage was written?' Imagine, for example, what might happen if you muddled up your love letter and your description to the police so that the police got the love letter!

There is more to reading the Bible than taking each word literally, at face value. That could lead to all kinds of misunderstanding. When Jesus said, 'I am the vine,' he did not mean it literally! And it is even more important not to take poems literally. They are full of picture language.

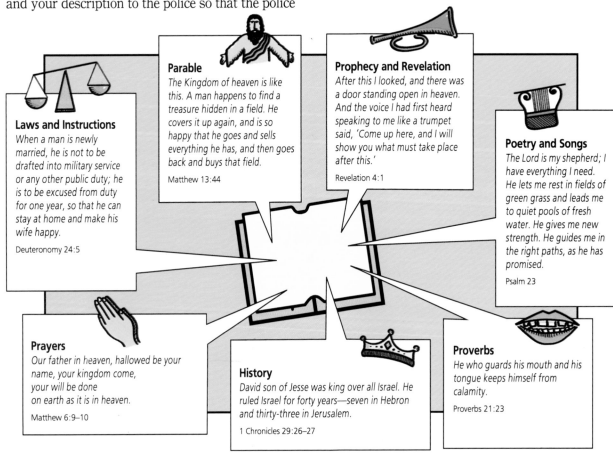

Laws and Instructions
When a man is newly married, he is not to be drafted into military service or any other public duty; he is to be excused from duty for one year, so that he can stay at home and make his wife happy.

Deuteronomy 24:5

Parable
The Kingdom of heaven is like this. A man happens to find a treasure hidden in a field. He covers it up again, and is so happy that he goes and sells everything he has, and then goes back and buys that field.

Matthew 13:44

Prophecy and Revelation
After this I looked, and there was a door standing open in heaven. And the voice I had first heard speaking to me like a trumpet said, 'Come up here, and I will show you what must take place after this.'

Revelation 4:1

Poetry and Songs
The Lord is my shepherd; I have everything I need. He lets me rest in fields of green grass and leads me to quiet pools of fresh water. He gives me new strength. He guides me in the right paths, as he has promised.

Psalm 23

Prayers
Our father in heaven, hallowed be your name, your kingdom come, your will be done on earth as it is in heaven.

Matthew 6:9–10

History
David son of Jesse was king over all Israel. He ruled Israel for forty years—seven in Hebron and thirty-three in Jerusalem.

1 Chronicles 29:26–27

Proverbs
He who guards his mouth and his tongue keeps himself from calamity.

Proverbs 21:23

The resurrection of Jesus

All four Gospels tell the same basic story. It was daybreak on Sunday when Mary Magdalene came to the tomb to anoint Jesus' body with spices. However, the tomb was empty and the stone had been rolled away. Jesus had risen from the dead and later that day was seen by Mary and by ten of the twelve disciples (Matthew 28:1–10; Mark 16:1–8; Luke 24:1–11; John 20:1–18).

Sometimes Christians disagree on how literally a passage is meant to be understood. A particularly important example of this is the story of the resurrection of Jesus.

The traditional approach is that the Bible is not to be taken word for word in a literal sense. You need to understand what type of literature you are reading. However, the Bible is a reliable source of information. What it says should be accepted as true. In this case it is accepted that the writers might have heard different versions of the same story. The important thing is that all the writers are saying the resurrection actually happened.

66 The resurrection is the starting point of Christianity. Every part of the New Testament throbs with the conviction that Jesus Christ was raised by God to life. 99

ARCHBISHOP GEORGE CAREY

The liberal approach holds that the Bible writers were inspired by God but could have made mistakes. People have to read the Bible critically: it cannot be taken at face value. Speaking of the resurrection David Jenkins (former Bishop of Durham) voices the liberal approach:

66 I don't think it means a physical resurrection, it means a spiritual resurrection. 99

The significance for him is the change in the mental attitudes of the disciples—they had an experience of the risen Jesus.

Brain Engage

1 Look up the following passages. Which type of writing is each? Exodus 20; Amos 5:21–27; Revelation 21; Psalm 96; 1 Kings 1:11–35; Matthew 1.

2 List the points of agreement between the traditional and the liberal approach.

3 What do you think about the resurrection story? Which viewpoint would you take? Give your reasons.

Summary

The Bible is made up of many different types of writing. To understand it the reader must think what the writer was trying to say.

The Big Change

Look at this photo. What are the people so excited about?

Some people have a great effect on others. Sport and pop stars have many fans who follow them. Some change their whole lifestyle to be like their 'hero'. Not all 'heroes' set their fans a good example, however.

For six years Dave Goerlitz worked as a model for Winston cigarettes. Earning over $2,000 a day Dave wasn't too concerned about the effects his work was having on other people. Then one day he visited his brother, who was dying of cancer in hospital.

66 I wasn't really the hero I thought I was. That's when I realised what I was doing and I made a decision to quit. 99

That was July 1989. Now Dave has swapped his role as a highly-paid model for charity work, warning children of the danger of the product he was once so successful in promoting.

'Follow me!'

Jesus' first public words challenged people to change their way of life and follow him: 'Turn away from your sins and believe the Good News!' (Mark 1:15).

Jesus called people to a new start. He told one man, Nicodemus, that he needed to be 'born again' (John 3:3). During his life, many people were magnetically drawn to follow him. Throughout the history of Christianity, millions of people have heard this call to change. The word they use to describe this experience is 'conversion'. It means a big change—a real turnaround, not just turning over a new leaf—like, for example: 'I've been converted from eating meat to being a vegetarian.' Sometimes conversion is a sudden, dramatic experience, at other times it is quite gradual.

At an open-air meeting in Chile a member of the audience experienced a dramatic change as he heard the good news of Jesus. He went up to the speaker and, to demonstrate his desire to change, he handed over his suitcase. Inside were a machine-gun and a bomb.

66 There's no one point at which I can say that I became a Christian—I was brought up one by my parents. When I look back over the years I can see small ways in which I have changed. Some things I find easier now than others. For example, I always try to tell the truth. However, I still find it difficult not to swear, especially when people get me angry. 99

ADEEBA, 15

Profile: Kriss Akabusi

Kriss Akabusi, international athlete and gold medal winner, became a committed Christian in 1986. In his climb to fame Kriss sought success through money and popularity. These were the only two things really important to him. However, 'No sooner than I'd got something, there was something else I wanted. I began to think that there had to be another meaning to life.'

Then, at the Commonwealth Games in Edinburgh in 1986, Kriss found a New Testament in his hotel room. In it he read about a man, the like of whom he had never met before. This was a man with power. He healed the incurably ill, walked on water, multiplied food, and even raised the dead. This was a man who was popular. Huge crowds followed him wherever he went. This was a man who was brave. He fearlessly criticized the authorities and calmly faced his Roman executioners. This was a man who was tough and yet gentle. This was a man who believed in his mission so completely that he gave up all home comforts, family and personal ambition to fulfil it. This was a man who was prepared to die.

'When I realized all these things about him, I just knew I had a decision to make. I started investigating to find out if what he said was true.

One night, a few months later, I simply prayed: "Lord, if you are there, and I really don't know if you are, you'd better come and say 'Hi' to Kriss."

And God did. 'I stopped having to prove that I was as good as everyone else.' A fellow athlete, Roger Black, noticed the difference in the new Kriss: 'No longer did he need to show off. He had peace in himself. His relationship with his wife Monika became stronger, he gave her more time.'

Summary

Christian conversion involves a complete turnabout: a commitment to follow Jesus in every part of life.

Brain Engage

1 Write down a list of ways in which you would like to change. Think about ways in which you can make changes in yourself. Would these changes be easy to make? Share your thoughts with a friend.

2 Draw/design a postcard that illustrates the story of someone whose life is completely changed when they become a Christian—it could be a cartoon card or a symbolic picture.

3 Look up the story of Nicodemus (John 3:1–6). Design a strip cartoon to illustrate the story. It should bring out what is said about change.

4 *Kriss Akabusi*

4a What impressed Kriss about Jesus?

4b How do you react to his story?

What's the Cost?

To be an athlete involves serious training. It costs a lot of time and effort to be successful. The training plan will cover every part of the athlete's life—what to eat and drink, as well as the hours of sleep, work and other habits.

5.30	Up early, light breakfast
6.00	At gym—training
7.00	Shower, change, home
7.30	Breakfast
8.00	School
12—1.00	Lunch hour: weight training session
1—3.30	Afternoon lessons
4.00	Home for light tea
5.00—8.00	Gym—training
8.30	Evening meal
9.30	Bed (early start tomorrow)

Being a Christian isn't quite like this, but Christians throughout the centuries have found that there is a cost to following Jesus.

Jesus warned his disciples that following him would not be easy:

❝ If anyone wants to come with me he must forget self, carry his cross, and follow me. For whoever wants to save his own life will lose it; but whoever loses his life for me and for the gospel will save it. ❞

MARK 8:34–35

He doesn't mean that all his followers will be martyrs. But putting Jesus first and self last can be tough.

❝ Being set apart from everybody else is difficult: you can feel really lonely. ❞

PENNY, 15

❝ Following Jesus is not like taking a leisurely Sunday stroll. It is more like an Everest expedition. [Being a Christian is] difficult but not impossible, because Jesus himself is with us, helping us over the difficult places. ❞

RICHARD HOLLOWAY, BISHOP OF EDINBURGH

❝ I feel it's very hard in school because you want to be popular and you have to a certain extent to sacrifice your popularity. ❞

KATHY, 17

What do you think Kathy and Penny are referring to?

❝ I remember I used to have this Bible—a little one. I used to love it. I had it in my bag for some reason. And there was a few boys and they wanted to borrow a pencil and they went to my bag and found the Bible. They thought it was really funny and said, "Oh yes, what is this? What are you going to do, pray and sing hymns?" So they started skitting me. ❞

ANGELINA

80

Brain Engage

1 The apostle Paul compared the Christian life to that of an athlete. Look up what he said in 1 Corinthians 9:24–27.

2 What do you think a Christian teenager would find most difficult in trying to keep their faith?

3 Why might a person need to change certain aspects of their lifestyle on becoming a Christian?

4 How do you react to Nikolai's story? Talk about this as a class.

Life situation: Nikolai Rublenko

Nikolai Rublenko was a bright, gifted teenager, a good swimmer who produced the top science project in his class. He could enjoy all the benefits which the old Soviet state could offer. But not, at that time, without giving up his faith.

Peter Blackmore worked with Nikolai's father to smuggle Bibles into Russia. If Nikolai informed on him to the secret police he could do really well for himself and be picked for all the teams. Instead, he went to meet Peter in the park.

'Where's your father?' asked Peter, when he met Nikolai.

'He can't make it. They're all being watched. I have come to take the Bibles.'

'You're just a boy,' Peter replied. 'Do you have any idea of how dangerous it is? No, I can't have you risking your life.'

'When a person gives his life to the Lord, Peter Blackmore, does he not give it all? Does he not give his whole life?' So Nikolai took the Bibles and gave them to other Christians, despite the danger.

Summary

To be a Christian involves challenge. It has many plus points, but can also be costly.

Where Am I Going?

Some people talk of life in terms of a journey from the cradle to the grave. Each journey is different, because we all have different experiences which affect us. Julie has started to draw the journey along the road of her life. You will notice that she has included the important events—and the people—that have helped make her into the person she is today. Some of these experiences she has chosen herself. Other things have simply happened to her. She has also included the things she wants to do in the future—her dreams and hopes. Look at her journey carefully. What does it tell you about Julie? What type of person do you think she is becoming?

- Draw your own life journey so far, marking on the important things which have happened to you. Try to think how these events have affected your life.

- Who have been the most important people in your life?

- Have you been influenced by anyone famous—on television for example?

- What good things have happened?

- What bad things have happened?

- What important decisions have you made?

- Also put in dream clouds the hopes you have for the future—what would you like to do in your life?

- You could also include what you think about dying one day—does it make you scared?

- Do you think there is anything after death?

Favourite school pudding—rice pudding and prunes.

Born in Spalding, Lincolnshire, 15.12.81

Discover I have an older brother and sister. Move to Manchester.

Age 6. Start to play the piano. Enjoy it.

Play rounders for school. Really like my Primary School teacher.

We win the Junior Schools Rounders Trophy.

Start at my new school! Very nervous!

Best holiday: swimming in Austrian lakes and eating huge cakes and strawberries all summer, age 12.

Join Christian Union. Arguing is fun!

A pilgrim people

The early Christians called themselves 'followers of the Way'. For them, one of the important things about the journey through life was that they had a companion. The 'Way' they were following was the person Jesus, who called himself 'The way, the truth and the life' (John 14:6).

Christians believe that they are on a journey with a purpose. Jesus showed them the way to God. Christianity is not about believing a list of things. It is an invitation to follow Jesus. Parts of this journey may be easy but other parts may be very hard. However, Christians believe they have a travelling companion, Jesus, who will guide them. Throughout life Christians try hard to become more and more like Jesus. It is a gradual process of change.

66 I sort of look back and see how far I've come and what's happened in the last year. The way Jesus is taking more of me. You can see different patterns of thought... **99**

ANNE

Although Christians can't see the details of the future they do have a clear idea of their final destination.

Do OK at school. Not mega-brill. Enjoy sport, art and English lessons.

Decide to get baptized—dunked in a pool in the church.

I am in love!

Brain Engage

1 Julie's life is a mixture—things she has chosen herself, and experiences over which she has had no control. Make a list of four things which you have chosen so far (for instance, friends) and four things which are out of your control (such as your choice of parents).

2 Test yourself. What sort of person are you becoming?

2a Do you find it easier to:
- love or hate
- give or take
- forgive or hold grudges
- like people or dislike people
- make friends or enemies
- think about yourself or others?

2b What do you think is the most important thing to achieve in life:
- a good job
- a family
- a lot of money
- something else (add your own goal)?

2c How often do you ask big questions about life, such as: 'Who am I?' 'Where am I going?' 'What is the purpose of life?' 'What happens when I die?':
- all of the time
- quite a lot
- sometimes
- very rarely
- never?

3 What do you think the following saying means? 'The future lies before you like a sheet of driven snow; Be careful how you tread it, for every step will show.'

4 Read the story of the rich young man in Matthew 19:16–30. What was the young man's aim in life? Why did Jesus ask him to give up his riches? What was the man's response? Why do you think he reacted in this way?

Summary

Christians believe that life is a journey with a purpose. Jesus is their guide and the Bible is their guidebook.

What Should I Do?

Study each of the following situations. With a partner
(a) describe what you would do if you were there
(b) explain your reasons.
How do you decide?

Do you

● walk past

● give money

● talk to the person

● give food?

Brain Engage

1 In groups, discuss how you make your decisions on how to act. The following suggestions may help you:
  ● I must always be honest
  ● I must always look after number one—ME.
  ● I must always be loyal to friends.

2 Some people base their decisions on keeping rules. Make a list of any rules that you follow. Which ones do you have to follow and which do you choose to follow?

3 Are rules a good thing? Think of a rule of the road (for example 'Always stop at Give Way signs'). What would it be like if the rule was removed?

4 How do we learn what is right or wrong? Prioritize the following list explaining what influences us most: parents, friends, TV, school, church, books, computer games.

Do you

● go to the rescue

● talk to an adult

● ignore it?

Do you

● tell on your friend

● confront your friend

● do something else?

Under new management

Jesus did not give his followers a new rule book to live by. Instead he called his disciples to put their trust in him and to follow his example of a life based on love. He told them to love God and to love other people.

In a football team you have to keep the rules of the game but that's not enough. Team members need to get into the habit of doing what the manager wants them to do. Christians get into the habit of asking 'how would Jesus have handled the situation?'

In his Sermon on the Mount (Matthew 5—7), Jesus gave his disciples a clear idea about what this would mean in practice. Here are some examples:

- Do for others what you want them to do for you (Matthew 7:12).

- Do not judge others ... for God will judge you in the same way as you judge others (Matthew 7:1–2).

- Love your enemies and pray for those who persecute you! (Matthew 5:43–44).

- Do not take revenge on someone who wrongs you. If anyone slaps you on the right cheek, let him slap your left cheek too (Matthew 5:39).

Jesus is asking the impossible! But Christians believe they are under new management—which means a clean slate, a new start and help from God to live this new life of love.

66 There's lots of little things. Such as when you're saying horrible things about your brother and then you realize that's stupid and you shouldn't really think things like that. Or I don't want to do something but I know I should, so I do. I don't know what I'd be like if I didn't have this consciousness behind me that God doesn't want me to do that. Temptation keeps coming in. 99

MANDY

Mary explains how trying to live as a Christian affects her:

66 Sometimes there's ways you want to behave and you realize there's ways that Jesus would prefer you to behave. I find when I give the loving answer, rather than the selfish or nasty answer, it's so much more peaceful and fulfilling. 99

Brain Engage

5 Design an Identikit of a disciple by

- drawing the outline of a person on a large sheet of paper

- using Matthew 5—7 to pick out sayings which show what a disciple is to do/be or not to do/be.

Summary

The Christian life is based on Jesus' command to love God and other people, which means following his example.

Love Is All You Need

Jesus taught that his followers should stand out from the crowd by the way they loved other people. But what did he mean?

The people in the photographs all use the word love. But are they talking about the same thing?

> **I would do anything for you.**

> **I still love her, but she has to be punished.**

> **I just love hamburgers.**

What is love? Is it made up of a whole lot of ingredients? Look at what Paul says in 1 Corinthians 13:

Love: the right ingredients

● **Love is ...** very patient * kind * puts up with a lot

● **Love does not ...** demand its own way * hold grudges * keep pointing out others' wrongs.

● **Love is never ...** jealous * envious * boastful * proud * selfish * rude * irritable * touchy.

⌖ Brain Engage

1 As a class, brainstorm all the different ways in which the word love is used.

2 Try putting your own name in place of the word 'love' in the ingredients list above. How far can you get without feeling uncomfortable?

3 Take each of the words in the ingredients list for love and say what it means. For example, 'Boasting is ... when a person tries to look big—to give the impression that they are better than other people.' You could do this in cartoons.

4 Design a LOVE IS ... poster and display it.

5a Write at the top of a large sheet of paper: 'How to get my own way.' Make a list of ways in which people get their own way, for example, by nagging or tricking you.

5b On another piece of paper, write: 'How to show selfless love.' Put down all the ways people can show love in a selfless way, for example, by giving more and taking less.

6 Make your own poem based on 'Love isn't ...'

Love costs

Christians believe that the ability to love like this comes from God. Totally unselfish love does not come naturally: they have to ask God to help them change.

Obeying the command to love, and following Jesus' example is often a struggle. It can also be very costly as the story of the young Polish priest, Jerzy Popieluszko illustrates. As a Christian he knew he must show love to his enemies who were trying to kill him.

One Christian teenager talks about how her attitudes have changed:

66 I could quite easily smack people in the mouth. I stand there and I say to myself: "No, I'm a Christian, so I shouldn't." But I'd really like to plant them one, and I have to keep saying to myself, "No, I cannot hit you because I love you." 99

Life situation: Jerzy Popieluszko

1945: At the end of the Second World War Poland was taken over by Communist Russia.

In 1980 Polish workers rose in revolt against the Communists.

13 December 1981: Martial law was imposed and Solidarity supporters were arrested.

The church in Poland began to speak out—to tell the world what was happening. One of the priests to do this was Jerzy Popieluszko.

The more Jerzy spoke out, the more the government started to think this man was a threat. But Jerzy continued to speak out.

He took soup to the shivering soldiers who were spying on him.

On 19 October 1984 he was kidnapped by the secret police, beaten and thrown to the bottom of a dam.

Summary

Christians believe they must obey Jesus' command to love—even though it can be costly.

This Glue Mends People!

MEGAN, I THOUGHT YOU WERE MY FRIEND. DID YOU HAVE TO OPEN YOUR BIG MOUTH AND TELL THE WHOLE SCHOOL MY SECRETS? I'LL NEVER EVER TRUST YOU AGAIN...I'LL NEVER FORGIVE YOU.

Brain Engage

1 In groups discuss the picture strip. What would you do if a friend betrayed you like this:

- keep quiet and then tell all your friends her secrets?

- pretend it didn't happen because you don't want to lose your friend, but nevertheless feel very hurt?

- confront her quietly and try to talk about it without losing your temper?

- forgive and forget?

- have a big row and only 'make friends' if she grovels?

2 Make a list of all those things which you would find most difficult to forgive. For example, could you forgive somebody who stole something from you, or somebody who hurt someone you loved?

The 'glue' in the title is love. And love that 'mends' involves forgiving.

To forgive somebody is to let go of our anger and hurt, to refuse to pay people back for what they have done to us. Forgiveness is the glue that mends a broken relationship.

Christians believe that because God in his love has forgiven them, they must forgive others. Loving others means we will forgive them. It rules out revenge.

Some things are easier to forgive than others. One of the most difficult things of all to forgive is murder. But that is what Gordon Wilson did when his daughter died as a result of a terrorist bomb.

It was 8 November 1987. The people of Enniskillen gathered for their Remembrance Day service at the cenotaph. It never took place. Shortly before 11 a.m. an IRA bomb blew up killing eleven people. One of them was Marie Wilson, a twenty-one-year-old nurse. Her father, Gordon Wilson, held hands with her under a mound of rubble, as she became unconscious. She died hours later in hospital. When Gordon Wilson was interviewed on television he said:

❝ I have lost my daughter, and we shall miss her. But I bear no ill will, I bear no grudge. Dirty sort of talk is not going to bring her back to life. Our Lord taught us to pray, "Forgive us our sins, as we forgive those who sin against us." We ask God to forgive us, but we must forgive others. When I think of the people responsible for killing Marie I don't bear them nasty thoughts. As human beings they have their own pieces to pick up. They will ultimately have to face their God, as I will. I still pray for the bombers. ❞

Brain Engage

3 Imagine that you were Gordon Wilson. What would you be feeling? Do you think Gordon Wilson was right to forgive the IRA terrorists?

4 Jesus taught a lot about forgiveness. Look up the following passages and make a list of things which Jesus said: Matthew 5:38–39; Matthew 5:43–45; Matthew 18:21–35.

5 Jesus himself forgave his murderers—look up Luke 23:34 and find out why. Christians believe that if they follow Jesus they must be prepared to forgive in the same way.

Extra

6 With a partner, imagine a situation when trust in a friendship is broken. One of you has to forgive the other. How will you work out the situation? Discuss it and act it out.

7 Write your own caption starting with the words, 'Forgiveness is . . .'

STUDENT'S PARENTS FORGIVE AS KILLER GETS LIFE SENTENCE

How can people forgive the horrible things done against them?

A Dutch woman, Corrie Ten Boom, suffered under the Nazis in Ravensbruck concentration camp during the Second World War. In the camp she saw her sister Betsie die. As a Christian she knew that she had to obey Jesus' command to forgive . . . but how was she to do it?

In her book *Tramp for the Lord* she says what forgiveness means to her:

> 66 When we confess our sins God casts them into the deepest ocean, gone forever. I believe God then places a sign out there that says, NO FISHING ALLOWED. Forgiveness is not just a thought. It also requires action. To forgive is not to forget the evil done, nor to say it was not someone's fault. It is to give up the right to go on blaming and hating. 99

One day after the war an ex-guard turned up at a church service where Corrie was preaching. He asked her to forgive him.

> 66 I stood there—I whose sins had again and again to be forgiven by God—and I could not forgive. I stood there with the coldness clutching my heart. "Jesus help me!" I prayed silently. "I can lift my hand. You supply the feeling." And so I thrust my hand into the one stretched out to me. And as I did, an incredible thing took place. The current started in my shoulder, raced down my arm and this healing warmth seemed to flood my whole being. I had never known God's love so intensely as I did then. 99

Corrie was able to forgive because God gave her the power to do so.

Summary

Love, for Christians, means forgiving the hurts and wrongs done to them.

Love In Action

Look carefully at the picture. What do you see?

What would you do if you walked into this situation?

What qualities would you need in order to help?

Jesus' example

Christians believe that Jesus has given them a special command to love all people—and that means action. In John's Gospel Jesus says: 'I give you a new commandment: love one another. As I have loved you, so you must love one another' (John 13:34).

Jesus went out of his way to love those whom other people rejected—the lepers, the prostitutes, cheating tax collectors . . . So Christians must meet the needs of others as Jesus did—they must not think anything or anyone beneath them.

In his Gospel Luke recounts that one day a teacher of the Law asked Jesus what he had to do to win eternal life. Jesus replied that to fulfil the Jewish law he must love God and love his neighbour as himself. When the man asked, 'Who is my neighbour?' Jesus answered by telling the story of the Good Samaritan (Luke 10: 30–37):

Today, Christians try to follow Jesus' example by meeting people's needs—in relief work (as in this TEAR Fund picture) and many kinds of service.

- A Jewish man was travelling from Jerusalem to Jericho when he was attacked by robbers. He was left for dead.
- Two Jewish religious leaders came along. When they saw the man they crossed the road and did not help.
- Eventually a Samaritan came along. He stopped and bandaged the man and paid for him to stay at an inn, till he was well.

What is important about this story?

- The Jews hated the Samaritans. It was the Samaritan, and not the two Jewish leaders, however, who helped the wounded man.
- The Jewish law stressed that you must show love to your neighbour. In the story the Jewish leaders, who should have upheld the Law, ignored this. The true neighbour was the Samaritan who showed love.
- The Samaritan, who was obviously rich, risked his own safety by stopping to help.

Brain Engage

1 Draw the story of the Good Samaritan in a series of cartoons, bringing out the feelings of the people involved.

Love in a box

Today, Christian groups throughout the world put love into practice by serving others in many different ways. One example of this is the link which has been formed between a church in Wrexham, England and churches all over Eastern Europe.

Operation Christmas Child began when Dave Cooke first saw the dreadful TV images of Romania's starving orphans in October 1990. Dave was determined to put his faith to practical effect.

Since 1990 convoys of lorries have travelled from Wrexham to Romania bringing food, clothes, medicines and aid. Although the convoys are busy all year around they call it Operation Christmas Child.

'We do what we do because of the first Christmas Child. The whole purpose of this is for children at home and abroad to rediscover the true meaning of the Christmas Child.'

Mark Swindley, one of the lorry drivers, explains how important it is for him to do this work:

'Regardless of how much you give out in Romania you receive so much more back. The love you receive from the children will get you home on its own! It is a real blessing to see the joy which you can give in such a short time. I feel that I am giving something back to God. I am doing God's work. I can't preach to save my life but I can drive a truck, carry boxes and give a bit of love whilst I'm here.'

Children stand in line at a refugee camp in Croatia. Many Christians are bringing practical help in difficult situations.

Christian Aid started in Britain after the Second World War as a response of the churches to help refugees throughout Europe who had been made homeless. Today it works all over the world, helping people to help themselves overcome drought, famine and other tragedies.

66 Christ has no body now on earth but yours, no hands but yours; no feet but yours. Yours are the eyes through which Christ's compassion is to look out on the world. Yours are the feet with which he is to go about doing good. Yours are the hands with which he is to bless others now. 99

TERESA OF AVILA (1515–82)

66 Non-Christians and Christians both do social work, but non-Christians do it for something, while we do it for someone. We do it for God. It is our love of God in action. 99

MOTHER TERESA OF CALCUTTA

Brain Engage

2 Explain why you think Dave Cooke called his work 'Operation Christmas Child'.

3 What do you think Saint Francis meant when he said, 'Go and preach the Gospel' and added, 'use words if necessary'?

4 Draw a cartoon of a situation where it would be really hard to show self-giving love. Give it the caption: 'Love must be tough.'

Extra

5 Can you see love? How can you see it? Describe one situation where you have recognized the kind of unselfish love Christians talk about.

6 Find out about the work of one of the aid agencies.

Summary

Christians show love by following the example of Jesus in serving others.

My Brothers and Sisters

A number of people with different skin colours were photographed with a heat-sensitive camera. Here are the pictures:

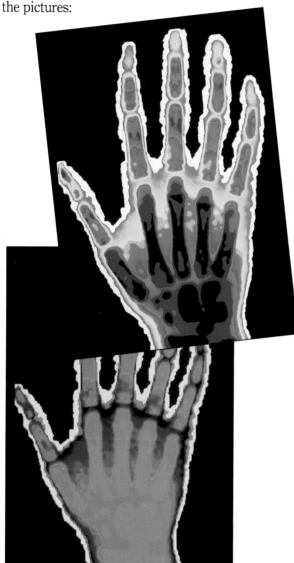

Although people look different on the outside, beneath the skin they are all the same. Christians believe that all people are of equal value in the eyes of God. They were created and are loved by God. We are all brothers and sisters and belong to one human family.

However, it is obvious from looking at any newspaper that all are not treated the same.

> **Who is black and who is white in these photos?**

> **Who is male and who is female?**

The Banquet

A charity working to help the hungry of the world organized a fund-raising banquet. Each guest paid the same amount for a ticket, although different coloured invitations were given out.

When the guests arrived at the banquet they found that one small table at the top of the room was laden with all sorts of rich food, whilst each of the other tables had only one communal bowl of rice. The guests with the pink tickets were served with wine by waiters. Those with white tickets were packed off to the other tables where they had to feed themselves from the single bowl of rice.

All the guests felt awkward. Those with pink tickets felt too embarrassed to tuck into their rich food whilst all the other guests had only rice to eat. Those with white tickets felt angry—after all, they had paid the same amount for their ticket.

Eventually the organizers pointed out that this was exactly the situation in the world today. A few rich countries enjoy plenty, while most of the world's people have very little.

⊙ Brain Engage

1 Make a montage entitled 'We are all one family

2 Design a file called 'Work Outstanding'. In this file make a list of all the work which still needs to be done in the world to make people more equal. You may like to cut things out of newspapers, magazines, advertising material from charities.

Extra

3 Find out about the work of Christian Aid.

It's only fair!

One country where there is a big divide between the rich and poor is Brazil. Although it is one of the richest countries in the world, over half of the population lives in poverty. Wages for poor people are at starvation level and most of the public money is spent on facilities for the rich.

Just outside the coastal city of Recife in Brazil is a rubbish tip. Poor people build little huts on the tip and spend all their time searching amongst the rubbish for anything which they can sell.

Brain Engage

4 Write a letter of complaint from Jesus to the people of Brazil.

5 Christian love means working for fairness and justice at home, too, in everyday situations. Look through a local newspaper. Make a list of stories where people are not being treated fairly. What could be done about the situation?

Christians believe that they are called to follow Jesus' example, and to stand on the side of the poor.

Over the last fifteen years in Brazil, over 120,000 new churches have been formed called base Christian communities. These churches are working to change people's lives for the better and to set people free from poverty.

But how are they changing people's lives?

- By making the poor aware that things can be improved

- By telling poor people that God really cares about them: all his life Jesus worked alongside the poor and the outcast

- By bringing people together to read the Bible, to pray and discuss what it has to say about their problems today

- By encouraging poor people to take action to persuade the government to give them better housing, proper wages and so on

- By setting up youth groups, clinics, dentists for the poor.

66 Jesus Christ the Liberator cared for the poor, the sick and the outcast. He is calling us to change things in our own lives, but also in our communities and our places of work. He is with us in our struggle. 99

TEREZINHA, MEMBER OF A BASE COMMUNITY

Summary

Christians believe that a commitment to love is a commitment to work for justice.

We All Need to Belong

We all need to belong. And in fact we all do belong to groups of one kind or another: the photos show a family group, a team, and a group of friends.

When we are left out of groups we feel hurt and lonely. What is it about belonging to groups which is so important? A sense of real belonging, of being accepted by others, affects our actions and how we feel about ourselves.

Brain Engage

1 Make a list of all the groups to which you belong: school, family . . .

2 Study the three photographs. Each shows a group of people who belong together. Write a caption for each photograph by completing the following sentence: 'Belonging to this group is important because . . .'

3 Look at the group of friends again. Notice the outsider. Have you ever been in a situation like that? What do you think it feels like? Write a short poem or story about what the person outside the group might feel. Call it 'The Outsider'.

4 Have you ever joined a group which has particularly impressed you? What was the most important thing about it?

The church as the family of God's people

The church is a worldwide group of people who belong together. However, unlike any other group, the church has been described as a club for outsiders. It does not exist just for those people who belong to it. Anyone can join: women and men; black, yellow, white; the poor and the rich. Jesus himself showed a special interest in all those people who were rejected by the rest of society, the hurt and the lonely. The church belongs together because each member belongs to Jesus.

The church of St Martin in the Fields, in the heart of London, provides day centres for the community, shelter and a soup kitchen for the homeless, and help in resettlement.

Brain Engage

5 Design a logo for the church which shows that it is a 'club for outsiders'.

6 How do you think Taizé and St Martin in the Fields would describe their roles?

One Christian community which seeks to live out the idea that the church is a worldwide family is Taizé.

Taizé was started by Brother Roger in 1940. It was a place of refuge for people fleeing the Nazis.

'I believed that it was essential to create a community which would seek to bring people together and to mend broken relationships.'

BROTHER ROGER

Today thousands of young people visit Taizé each week.

'They come to feel part of a church which reaches to all four corners of the earth. They are part of a large family, the worldwide family of God. When they leave Taizé they go out to be peacemakers, to mend broken relationships in their own neighbourhoods, to work for peace, hope and reconciliation.'

Summary

Christians believe that the church belongs to everyone. Anybody can join.

Belonging to a Body

Sometimes people use 'word pictures' to describe something. For example, have you ever heard people say, 'life's a bed of roses', 'you little monkey', or 'my mum's an angel'? Christians use a number of 'word pictures' from the Bible to describe the church. One of these is to say that the church is the 'body of Christ'.

For the human body to work properly every part must do its particular job. Our health depends on all the parts working together.

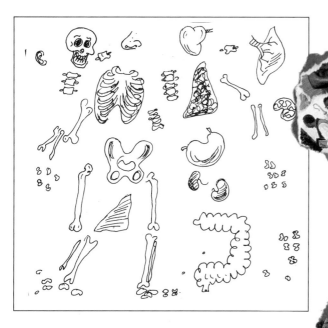

Descriptions of the church

● The body of Christ (1 Corinthians 12:27)

● God's fellow-workers (1 Corinthians 3:9)

● Light for the world (Matthew 5:14)

● God's own people (1 Peter 2:9)

● Salt for all humanity (Matthew 5:13)

● Soldiers of Christ Jesus (2 Timothy 2:3–4)

● Branches of the vine (John 15:5)

Paul calls the church the 'body of Christ'. By using this image he was saying that Christ is at the centre and that although there are many different types of Christians they are all joined together.

Christians work together in many different ways, bringing their own particular gifts to the body.

Eastern Orthodox Church

The Eastern Orthodox Church lays particular stress on this 'word picture' of the church as a body. The 'body' includes believers in heaven and on earth: a body that spans time as well as space. In worship, they believe that heaven and earth meet. The design of the church illustrates this:

In an Orthodox church everything has a meaning

The church is decorated with religious pictures (called icons) of saints: this reminds people that all Christians whether in heaven or on earth are gathered together to worship God.	*Ceiling = heaven—large icons of Jesus usually appear on the dome.*	*Floor = the world—most Orthodox churches do not have seats; people stand and move about during the services.*	*Iconostasis = a screen with icons: this divides the church in two, like heaven and earth; it produces a sense of holiness and awe.*	*The altar = God's throne—the climax of Orthodox worship is the celebration of the Eucharist on the altar: this is when heaven and earth are joined and all people, alive and dead, are united in Jesus.*

The picture above shows a Greek Orthodox church in London; right is a twelfth-century Russian icon of Christ and his virgin mother, Mary. When people enter Orthodox churches they kiss the icons as a sign of respect and devotion. The icons point to something beyond themselves. They are windows into heaven.

66 We talk to the saints as we would to the members of the Church on earth; we are all the Body of Christ and Jesus has broken down the barrier of death. We are all alive and part of God's family. **99**

COSTAS, A GREEK ORTHODOX DEACON

Brain Engage

1 Use this page to write your own paragraph on the Eastern Orthodox Church. What five facts would you include?

2 How does the Eastern Orthodox Church create a sense of mystery in its building and worship?

Summary

Christians describe the church as the body of Christ.

The Same Yet Different

Christianity started small, with just the twelve disciples Jesus chose. It soon spread. In 313 CE the Roman Emperor Constantine made it the official religion of the Empire. From there it spread until today there are Christians in almost every country of the world. They share a common belief, summed up in the creeds. All worship Jesus and try to live by his teachings. But this is worked out in different ways—especially of worshipping God and organizing the church.

Today there are as many as 20,000 groups that can be called 'denominations'. These denominations spring from three main branches of Christianity: Eastern Orthodox, Roman Catholic and Protestant. They are not different religions. Each is part of the whole Christian family and they have much in common. The following diagram shows the biggest groupings of churches in the Christian family today:

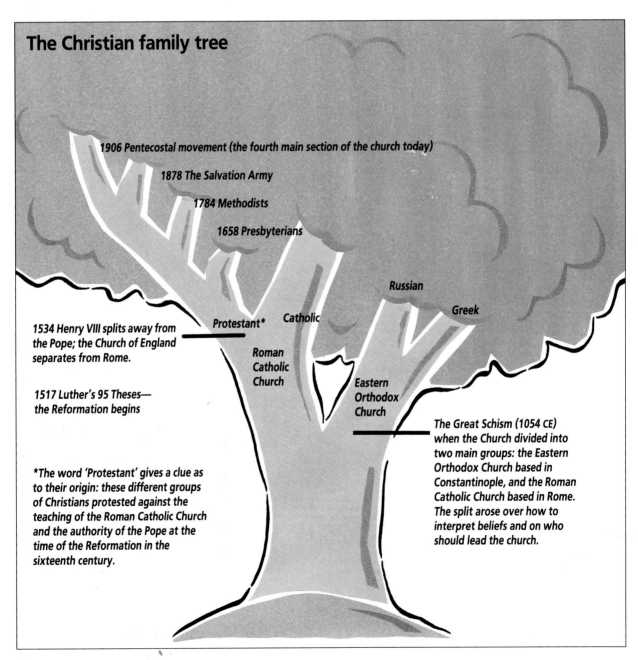

The Christian family tree

1906 Pentecostal movement (the fourth main section of the church today)

1878 The Salvation Army

1784 Methodists

1658 Presbyterians

Russian

Greek

Protestant*

Catholic

1534 Henry VIII splits away from the Pope; the Church of England separates from Rome.

Roman Catholic Church

Eastern Orthodox Church

1517 Luther's 95 Theses— the Reformation begins

The Great Schism (1054 CE) when the Church divided into two main groups: the Eastern Orthodox Church based in Constantinople, and the Roman Catholic Church based in Rome. The split arose over how to interpret beliefs and on who should lead the church.

*The word 'Protestant' gives a clue as to their origin: these different groups of Christians protested against the teaching of the Roman Catholic Church and the authority of the Pope at the time of the Reformation in the sixteenth century.

Talking heads

Roman Catholics

Gaelle (21), a Catholic, talks about her church and the Pope who is its head:

66 Two distinctive things about being a Roman Catholic are the importance of the Pope and Mary. Roman Catholics trace their history back to Peter, the disciple Jesus chose to lead the church. Peter took charge of the church in Rome. The Pope can traces his leadership back to Peter. He is our spiritual leader. For example, we are guided by the Pope's teachings on such moral issues as abortion, euthanasia.

'Mary is a very special person for us. She is the mother of Jesus, God's Son. Throughout her life she was the model disciple showing us what being a Christian means—being open to what God wanted of her at all times. We can pray to her and she will intercede for us to God. 99

Brain Engage

1 We all have our own family tree. Draw your family tree. Ask your parents to help you trace it back as far as possible. Write down two things which you have inherited from your parents and grandparents and two things which make you different from them. The Christian Church can both trace its history back and be seen to have developed.

2 Does it make sense to have a national Church in England when many different religions exist side by side?

Extra

3 What are the advantages and disadvantages of the church having different branches/denominations?

Eastern Orthodox Church

Costas (32), an Orthodox deacon, talks about his church:

66 We trace our history back to the beginnings of Christianity. The word "Orthodox" means "right glorification". We believe that we have worshipped (glorified) God in the correct way and kept safe the right belief since the time of Jesus. One thing you will notice if you come to our churches is the richness of worship: the beautiful icons, the singing, the incense.

'Within the Orthodox church there are a number of groups: Greek Orthodox, Russian Orthodox, Serbian Orthodox. We call our leaders "patriarchs", a word which means "father". 99

Church of England

This is England's state church. The Queen is called the 'Defender of the Faith'. The whole country is split up into parishes which include everyone whether they worship at the church or not. Many people choose to get married and have their funeral in the parish church.

At present there is a big debate whether the monarch should be the head of a particular church when the country is becoming more and more multi-cultural, with many different faiths.

Although different churches stress different parts of the faith, they are united by the basic Christian beliefs they share. The World Council of Churches, whose logo is shown above, was formed in 1948 to encourage the great branches of the Christian church to work together.

Summary

There are well over 20,000 different Christian groups. They are united in the beliefs they share.

Saints Alive!

Some people attract others to them, like a magnet attracting something made of metal.

Look carefully at the faces of the people in the photograph. Describe what the photograph is about. Make a list of the thoughts and feelings which might be going through the minds of the people in the photograph.

What is the effect of the pop star on the minds and lives of his followers?

We all have people we greatly admire. For some it may be a parent, or a teacher. For others it is someone more famous—maybe a pop star or a sports personality. We all need examples to follow. They inspire and encourage us.

The word translated as 'saints' in the New Testament means 'God's people'—those who follow Jesus and are determined to live as he wants them to. From earliest times, certain Christians have stood out as examples of what it is to follow Jesus with their whole hearts and minds.

Jesus told the story of a man who sold everything he had to buy the finest pearl (Matthew 13:45–46). In this parable he taught that a true follower of his would value their relationship with God above anything else. Again, in the Sermon on the Mount, Jesus praised those people who 'hungered' after goodness (Matthew 5:6).

Christians today are inspired by the example of such people. The church has recognized some of them by officially naming them as 'saints'. Some have been prepared to die for their beliefs. These people are called martyrs. Some of them are remembered on special days of the year. They are the heroes of Christianity.

You can often see pictures of saints in the stained-glass windows of churches. The light shines through them. The lives of the saints are like windows to God—they let God's light shine through them. Each illuminates a particular characteristic of God: his love for the poor, his justice...

66 'I will be a saint' means I will give up my own desires and give myself completely to God. 99
MOTHER TERESA

66 Saints are people who are very close to God. They make God near. This is the most marvellous thing that one human being can do to another. 99
MICHAEL RAMSEY

Saints are God's adverts in the world

People in El Salvador are divided between the very rich and the great majority of people who are very poor.

The government favoured the rich—they were corrupt and got rid of people who spoke out against them.

Oscar Romero courageously spoke out—he told the world what was happening in his country.

A modern martyr who gave his life for the poor: Oscar Romero (1917–80), Archbishop of El Salvador.

THIS WEEK 5 PEOPLE HAVE DISAPPEARED! INSTEAD OF KILLING INNOCENT PEOPLE THE GOVERNMENT SHOULD SHARE WHAT THEY HAVE

THE POOR ARE THE BODY OF CHRIST TODAY. THE RICH ARE TRAMPLING ON THE POOR

Oscar was threatened—his life was in danger. The rich were out to get him. A few days before his murder, he rang a reporter.

I HAVE OFTEN BEEN THREATENED WITH DEATH. HOWEVER, AS A CHRISTIAN I DO NOT BELIEVE IN DEATH WITHOUT RESURRECTION. AS A PRIEST I HAVE TO BE WILLING TO GIVE MY LIFE FOR THE POOR

On 25 March 1980 Oscar was saying Mass when suddenly a shot rang out—he slumped down dead in front of thousands of people in the church.

Today pilgrims visit his tomb and leave messages, cards and flowers.
'With Archbishop Romero God passed through El Salvador.'
'In Romero the whole church has been given a saint for our times.'

Brain Engage

1 Pick out those things in the description of Romero which suggest that he is a saint.

2a Who would you vote to be a saint? Whom do you particularly admire and why do you admire them?

2b As a class organize a balloon debate with four people each representing a particular 'saint'. You need to lighten the weight of the balloon which is falling to the ground. Which 'saint' would be the last to be tipped overboard? Why?

Oscar Romero's memory and example lives on . . .
'I believe that when I saw Oscar Romero and look at the way he lived and died I have seen Jesus.'
A fellow priest says:
'Meeting Romero in person was like meeting God.'
'Like Jesus he made the powerful frightened—he wasn't afraid to criticize them. He preached against hatred, violence and injustice.'

Summary

Christian saints are people who make God present for others. In their lives they reflect God's nature.

Telling the World

If you really believe in something, is it right to want to convert others to your viewpoint? Why do Christians try to spread their faith?

Jesus' last instruction to his disciples after he had risen from the dead was: 'Go to all peoples everywhere and make them my disciples' (Matthew 28:19). Christians ever since have seen it as their task to spread the good news of Jesus. This is called 'missionary' work. Christianity is a missionary religion.

One Christian explained it this way:

> 66 Imagine that you had discovered a cure for AIDS. You would want to tell other people about your discovery as soon as possible. This is how Christians feel about Jesus' message. 99
>
> MARSHA, 22

The good news can be shared one-to-one, within groups by teaching and preaching, by gathering crowds to hear a speaker, by radio, film and television—in any number of ways.

Someone else has described what it means to spread the good news as 'one beggar telling another beggar where to find bread'.

One of the more eye-catching ways of 'telling the world' is by marching through the streets, singing and giving out leaflets to tell people about Jesus.

On 25 June 1994, 171 countries and an estimated ten million people took part in one of the largest religious events of all time: the first Global March for Jesus.

'We are marching for Jesus because he has been good news for us. He has changed our lives. He shows the way to harmony between people, and justice. We are marching because we believe you have a right to know that God is not dead, nor is his church.'

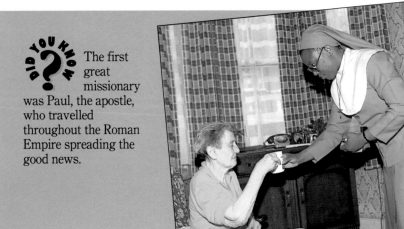

DID YOU KNOW? The first great missionary was Paul, the apostle, who travelled throughout the Roman Empire spreading the good news.

Along with the good news of Jesus missionaries have brought many good things to the countries they have travelled to. In Asia they have provided relief at times of famine and flood, and in many places medical missions continue to provide health care. Here a Nigerian missionary comes to London.

Christianity: a world faith

Because Christians have obeyed Jesus' command Christianity is now a world faith. Today there are more Christians in Latin America, Asia and Africa than in Western Europe. Today, the Roman Catholic Church is importing priests from Latin America to come and work in Western Europe.

In Britain today fewer people go to church each Sunday than they did even thirty years ago. In 1993 *The Guardian* newspaper asked five national advertising agencies to put together campaigns to get people back to church. The following posters were two of the results:

> What is each poster trying to say about the Christian message?

> How effective do you think they are?

Does your child believe that when you die, you go to Heaven, Hell or Level 3?

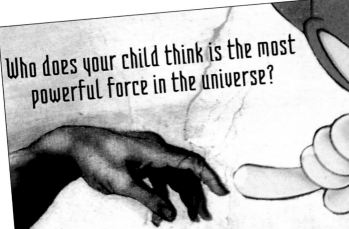

Who does your child think is the most powerful force in the universe?

America has taken the lead in 'selling' Christianity via the television. Tele-evangelists have their own channels on cable and satellite. Their programmes are showbiz productions.

66 *In a single telecast I preach to millions more than Christ did in his lifetime.* 99

BILLY GRAHAM

Brain Engage

1 Jesus told a parable about the importance of hearing the good news and then spreading it. Read the parable of the Sower in Mark 4:1–9. What is Jesus trying to teach in this parable?

2 Do you think television is a good way of spreading the Gospel? What type of programme do you think is most/least effective?

3 If you had the job of selling Christianity today, how would you go about it? Design your own advertisement for the Christian faith which you hope would bring people to church. Don't forget to give it a short title.

Summary

From the early days Christians have obeyed Jesus' command to spread the good news.

That's a Miracle!

What is a 'miracle'? Write your answer and compare it with that of your neighbour. Exchange ideas in class and come up with a definition. See if you want to change it at the end of the lesson.

In God's spotlight

What Christians describe as a miracle is something quite extraordinary—God intervening and apparently overruling the laws of nature. In the New Testament many miracles are described: rising from the dead; a blind man who gains his sight; water turned into wine...

Miracles were an important part of Jesus' work. He healed people, making them whole in body, mind and spirit. In the synagogue at Nazareth Jesus summed up his work by quoting from the book of the Old Testament prophet Isaiah:

66 The Spirit of the Lord is upon me, because he has chosen me to bring good news to the poor. He has sent me to proclaim liberty to the captives and recovery of sight to the blind; to set free the oppressed and announce that the time has come when the Lord will save his people. 99

LUKE 4:18–21

Today the church continues Jesus' healing work, in the main through Christians involved in medical treatment and research. There is also a ministry of healing and deliverance.

There are many opinions about miracles, both those of Jesus and miracle claims today. Here are two:

God created the laws of nature. But at times he intervenes in nature for a special reason.

All of Jesus' miracles can be explained by modern science.

The church's ministry of healing

Eva Roth had suffered from severe back pains for many years when she experienced physical healing through prayer:

66 It all happened about nine years ago. I had been suffering from severe bouts of backache which often made it impossible for me to work and even dress myself properly. Then one day when I was at church Ian Andrews (a healer) asked me to come forward and sit on a straightbacked chair. He told me to concentrate on Jesus and stretch out both of my legs. At that time one was shorter than the other. He held my feet and began to pray for one leg to be lengthened. I felt a sound like a dentist's drill and quite quickly both legs were the same length. From that moment on my back pains disappeared. I was cured. 99

EVA ROTH

Brain Engage

1 Jesus' healing miracles
Look up one of the following healing miracles of Jesus. Sit in pairs, back to back. Without talking, write a script of the event by passing a piece of paper back and forth. Include the feelings of the person before, during and after the healing.

- The paralysed man (Mark 2:1–12)
- Jairus' daughter and the woman who touched Jesus' cloak (Mark 5:21–43)
- The blind man of Bethsaida (Mark 8:22–26)
- The centurion's servant (Luke 7:1–10)

2 Sometimes we say people are 'sick at heart'. What do you think this means? What might healing mean in these situations?

3 Have a short class debate on the motion that 'God no longer does miracles.'

Not all Christians experience physical healing when they pray for it. Roy Castle, the entertainer and host of Record Breakers, died after a two-and-a-half-year battle against lung cancer. For two years after his diagnosis, Roy lived life to the full, raising millions of pounds for a cancer research centre. When asked if he feared death, Roy joked: 'No, millions have done it and there's never been a complaint.'

In his dying days Roy Castle was convinced of a new life. He felt he had seen God and paradise. He told his wife, Fiona: 'It's so beautiful, don't hang around, darling, join me soon.' The instructions for his funeral were: 'No flowers, no fuss, no mourning, just lots of joy.'

The ministry of deliverance

There are a number of stories in the Gospels which tell how Jesus cast out evil spirits from people. One-third of the miracles in the first three Gospels are 'exorcisms' of this kind.

Today, within the Church of England, nearly every diocese has its adviser working in this way.

People understand the casting out of demons in different ways:

66 In each of the New Testament cases the evidence points to the patient having suffered from some form of mental illness. It is no longer posible for us to see them as the result of evil spirits. 99

DR J. KEIR HOWARD

66 Not all cases can be explained away by mental illness. There are cases where people are under the influence of an alien power who controls them which cannot just be treated by medicine. Possession is brought about by deliberately choosing evil. 99

DOUGLAS HOWELL-EVERSON

Even after the cancer treatment which lost him his hair, Roy Castle went on campaigning for others.

Brain Engage

4 Jesus' exorcisms
Look up one of the following exorcisms Jesus performed:

- The madman in the tombs (Mark 5:1–20)

- Jesus heals a dumb man (Matthew 9:32–34).

What happens? What are people's reactions?

5 Who do you agree with: J. Keir Howard or Douglas Howell-Everson? Why?

Summary

Christians believe that God works through his church today to heal people and to deliver them from the power of evil.

Can We Talk?

Every relationship needs good communication. We get to know people by spending time with them, talking together. The Christian life is based on a relationship with God. Prayer is the way Christians communicate with God. As one Christian puts it:

66 He's the best friend you'll ever have, and he loves a good chat! 99

D. GATWARD

What is the person doing? How do you know?

What feelings do you associate with this photograph?

What questions would you want to ask the person in this photograph?

Christians believe that prayer is an essential part of life. Just as daily food is needed to build a strong and healthy body so Christians believe that daily prayer helps to feed the spirit.

Prayer is keeping in touch with base. People can use formal written prayers—or normal conversation:

66 Lord, are you there? Have you got time for a chat? Well, I just need to talk, I've a few questions. 99

66 Have you got a minute? It's just that I'm feeling down, and I don't know why. 99

In the Gospels Jesus is often described as praying to God. He would pray alone early in the morning. He sometimes went into the hills to be quiet. He prayed when he had a major decision to make: choosing the twelve apostles, for example, and in Gethsemane before he was to die (Mark 14:32–42).

One day when Jesus had finished praying one of the disciples said to him, 'Lord, teach us to pray.' Jesus said to them, 'When you pray, say this:

66 Our Father in heaven, hallowed be your name, your kingdom come, your will be done, on earth as in heaven. Give us today our daily bread. Forgive us our sins, as we forgive those who sin against us. Lead us not into temptation but deliver us from the evil one. 99

MATTHEW 6:9–13 (NEW INTERNATIONAL VERSION)

This prayer, 'the Lord's Prayer', has been prayed by Christians ever since.

People can pray any time, anywhere; alone or in groups; silently or out loud; using set words or speaking the way we would to a friend.

Mother Teresa's Missionaries of Charity are famous for the work they do with suffering people throughout the world. Their work, like much other Christian work, is based on a life of prayer.

The day begins in silent prayer. 'The more we receive in our silent prayer, the more we can give in our active life. We can work, but we cannot do it without God's help.'

'We pray through our work, performing it with Jesus. Mother Teresa tells us to make every effort to walk in the presence of God, to see God in everyone you meet. In the streets, in the shelters, in all your work, you should always be praying with all your heart and all your soul.'

New 'recruits' for Mother Teresa's Missionaries of Charity.

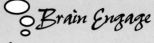

Brain Engage

1 Carefully look at the pictures on these pages. Write your own caption for each one, saying what is happening in each.

2 Why do you think Christians often pray with their eyes closed or looking down?

3a We use our bodies to express ourselves. What do the following mean: handshake; clapping; waving; bowing?

3b Gestures and hand positions are used in prayer too. Look at the photographs showing people in different prayer positions. What do you think the different postures express?

Extra

4 Read the following prayer: 'The guy next door is praying for a downpour on his garden and I'm praying just as hard for sunshine for my round of golf, so this is the crunch, Lord.'

- What view of prayer do these two people have?
- What problems are there in holding this view of prayer?
- How does this view of prayer differ from that presented in the opening lines of this section?

Summary

Prayer is the way Christians communicate with God.

Fans and Enthusiasts

What is the photograph about?

Why are the people behaving like this?

What might their feelings be?

Why do you think this person spends two hours in the gym each day?

What is the photograph saying about what is important to him?

What do you think is important to the couple in the photograph?

Draw a box in which you can put a photograph of yourself. Around the box, label all the things which are important to you, for which you sacrifice time and money.

The photographs show things which influence the lives of many people today. When people think something is important they will sacrifice money and time for it.

It could be said that these people are 'worshipping' what is important to them. The word 'worship' means 'giving something its worth or value'. It's by the things they reckon to be important that people show what they believe in. Worship expresses what people believe.

For Christians life is centred on Jesus. It is their relationship with God which makes their life worth living. They express their worship in many different ways, setting aside time for God on their own or together, trying to live as God wants, celebrating and praising God.

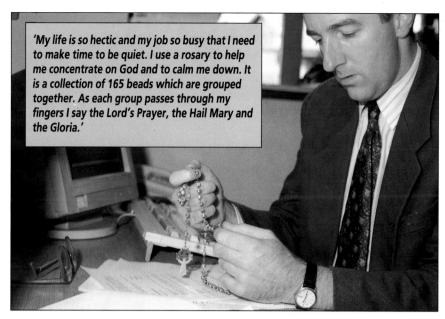

'My life is so hectic and my job so busy that I need to make time to be quiet. I use a rosary to help me concentrate on God and to calm me down. It is a collection of 165 beads which are grouped together. As each group passes through my fingers I say the Lord's Prayer, the Hail Mary and the Gloria.'

66 Jesus told us to remember him by eating the bread and drinking the wine. I feel really close to God when I obey his words. It is important that I share this meal with Christians all over the world—we are Christ's body on earth. 99

66 For me worship is about praising God. I want to show my love for God for all that he has done by singing and dancing. It's important that I praise God with all my body. By raising my hands in song I am opening all of my life to God. 99

66 When I have done things wrong I go to the priest to confess my sins. But first I must feel sorry about what I have done and really want to change. The priest forgives me on behalf of God. 99

66 When I want to say a special prayer for someone who is in trouble I light a candle. The light and the smoke which drifts upwards reminds me of prayers going to God. As the candle burns I think of the person who needs help. 99

'In our church the pulpit is central. The most important thing in worship is to hear the Word of God because we then know what God expects of us. He speaks to us through the Bible.'

Brain Engage

1 Look at the two photographs. They are both to do with 'worship'. Choose one of the photographs. Look at it quietly and try to imagine what the person is thinking and feeling. Write down what you think.

2 Look at the other photograph. Make a list of four questions you would like to ask this person about their worship.

3 Look at the photographs and quotations about Christians at worship. Make a list of the main differences in the styles of worship.

4 At the heart of worship is the desire to be open to God. Lie face downwards on the floor with your arms stretched out in front of you. What feeling(s) does it encourage?

Summary

Christians show their love for God by worshipping him, both in public and in private.

What's Life All About?

Three people have chosen a picture to show what they feel life is like. What picture would you draw?

From the cradle to the grave

Journey to the unknown

> I think life's one big adventure. You don't know exactly where you're going—that's half the excitement.

> I feel my life is like a conveyor belt. I can't get off. It's just one long line—going to school, getting a job, earning enough money to live on and then what...? Death at the end of the line.

I want to be happy

> I don't know what's going to happen in the future so I'm going to enjoy what I can when I can. As long as I'm happy, that's the only thing that's important.

Going somewhere?

Christians believe that life has a purpose: to love and serve God, which brings joy. They believe that life does not end with death; because Jesus has been raised from death those who believe can also look forward to a new life continuing beyond the grave.

One of the Bible's word-pictures shows life as a race, with God as the end goal. Paul tells the Christians in Corinth:

'Run your race to win... An athlete goes to all this trouble just to win a blue ribbon or a silver cup, but we do it for a heavenly reward that never disappears.'

1 CORINTHIANS 9:24–25
(LIVING BIBLE)

Welcome home!

Just before he died, Jesus told his disciples: 'Do not be worried and upset... There are many rooms in my Father's house, and I am going to prepare a place for you' (John 14:1–2).

This belief that life is going somewhere affects how Christians think about living and dying.

Garvan was 11 when he explained how he was facing up to his death, which he knew would happen soon:

66 When I was young, my mum told me about my illness and that I might die very soon. When she first told me, I have to say that I was a bit frightened. I'm not frightened any more. I think of my body as a reflection; it's how you recognize me. When I die I'll leave my reflection behind and it will fade. But the real ME won't die. The real ME is going to a very special place. Jesus said, I'm going to get somewhere ready for you; I'm going to prepare a place for you. There's so much to look forward to. 99

66 Death is not a full stop, it's a comma. If you look at the whole of life, death is an activity in the middle, it is not the end. 99

ELLEN WILKIE

66 The actual moment of dying is still a mystery. But I am not afraid. Jesus has already been through death, and will be with us when we walk through it ourselves. 99

DAVID WATSON,
just before he died of cancer

66 I'm not scared of dying. I'll be up with him, y'know. 99

Brain Engage

1 Which of the pictures on the left-hand page do you find (a) most appealing, (b) least appealing? Explain why.

2 Draw two small diagrams, one showing the view that life stops at death, the other that it goes on past the grave.

3 Some people say that if death is the end, then life has no meaning. Do you agree? Discuss this in class.

Extra

4 Check why Christians believe that life does not end with death. Read what Jesus said to Martha in John 11:25–26.

Summary

Christians believe that life does not end at death: Jesus has prepared a place for them.

What's the World Coming To?

Have you ever heard that saying before? People use it when they want to refer to the mess the world is in. Look around you—what do you see? Sometimes the end of the world seems just around the corner.

RWANDAN APOCALYPSE

The word 'apocalypse' refers to the world-shaking events at the end of time. This newspaper headline does not mean the world is literally coming to an end, but uses this dramatic word to underline the enormity of the disaster.

Brain Engage

1 Copy the box into your books.

1a In the first column list five things which are going wrong in the world.

1b In the second column say what the cause is of the things going wrong.

Things going wrong	Cause

Global warnings!

According to Christians we shouldn't be surprised by the way the world is. We were warned that disastrous things would happen way back—by Jesus.

Look carefully at the picture. Describe what you see. What goes through your mind when you look at it?

Most Christians wouldn't express their views in quite this way, but they do believe that the world will end one day.

The Bible says that the world will come to a sudden end, and Jesus will return to earth. He will then judge the world. The whole period between Jesus' life and his return to earth is called 'the last days' in the Bible. Jesus told people what to expect in this period:

- **International conflict**
  Instead of peace between nations there will be war and struggles.

- **Natural disasters**
  Jesus said that before he returned there would be famines and earthquakes.

- **Religious persecution**
  Christians will be persecuted and some will give up their faith in Jesus. (Christians have been persecuted ever since Jesus died.)

- **Religious fakes**
  There will be false religious leaders and many people will be taken in. (In this century there has been a growth of religious sects that have tried to influence people.)

The Christian hope

Although the world looks a mess now, Christians believe that this spoiled world will be remade:

> 66 We know that even the things of nature, like animals and plants, suffer in sickness and death as they await this great event. And even we Christians . . . also groan to be released from pain and suffering. We, too, wait anxiously for that day when God will give us our full rights as his children, including the new bodies he has promised us—bodies that will never be sick again and will never die. 99
>
> ROMANS 8: 22, 23 (LIVING BIBLE)

In Revelation (the last book of the Bible) there is a vision of this remade world:

> 66 I saw the Holy City . . . coming down out of heaven from God . . . I heard a loud voice speaking from the throne: "Now God's home is with mankind! He will live with them, and they shall be his people. God himself will be with them . . . He will wipe away all tears from their eyes. There will be no more death, no more grief or crying or pain. The old things have disappeared." Then the one who sits on the throne said, 'And now I make all things new!" 99
>
> REVELATION 21:2–5

However, Christians believe that before that can happen Jesus will return to judge the world and evil will finally be destroyed (see pages 114–15).

Brain Engage

2 If you knew the world was going to end in 48 hours what would you do? How would you change your life, if at all? Compare notes.

3 Read the following passages and make up your own banner warning people of the impending doom: Matthew 24; Luke 21:9, 11.

Summary

Christians believe that the world will come to a sudden end. Before then, there will be disasters and persecutions.

Looking to the Future

Throughout history there have been people who have called themselves the Messiah ('the Chosen One' God will send at the end of time). They attract followers. They say that the end of the world is near and that they have been sent to bring in the final judgment. Two people who believed this about themselves in recent years were David Koresh and Jim Jones.

Inferno ends Waco siege

Religious madman Dav Koresh and his followe were blown up last night. huge explosion rippe through their fortress i Waco, Texas. Inside were 9: people. Most are believed to be dead. David called himself the 'Lamb of God', and believed he was the Messiah. He had gathered around him a group of followers who believed he was the Second Coming of Christ sent by God to bring in the final judgment of the world.

Jim Jones leads 900 followers to mass suicide

As the US Army closed in, the Rev. Jim Jones commanded his followers to lie down and die. 900 men, women and children committed mass suicide in the forests of Guyana. Jones, who had set himself up as the Messiah, had persuaded his followers to take a lethal dose of cyanide, sleeping drugs and tranquillisers mixed in an orange drink.

What do you make of these events? Here are some people's views. What do you think?

> It's all a load of rubbish— they are all mad.

> There must be something in it for all those people to follow such leaders.

> The world is becoming so violent; it's no wonder that some people want to form a religious community preparing for the end.

Jim Jones and David Koresh got it wrong, but where did all this talk about a second coming come from? How does it affect people today?

Why do people believe Jesus will return?

- Jesus told his disciples: 'I will come back and take you to myself, so that you will be where I am' (John 14:3).

- The Bible ends with the promise that Jesus will come again: 'I am coming soon' (Revelation 22:20).

- However, it also teaches that before Jesus comes again there will be many who will falsely claim to be him: 'Many men, claiming to speak for me, will come and say, "I am he!", and they will deceive many people' (Mark 13:6, 22).

When will Jesus come?

> 66 No one knows when that day or hour will come ... only the Father knows. Be on watch. 99
>
> MARK 13:32–33

Jesus compared his return to that of a burglar. No thief sends a postcard saying when he is to rob a house. So Jesus will return when he is least expected (Matthew 24:42–44). People must always be ready.

What will Jesus do?

The Bible makes it clear that Jesus will return in glory to end human history and to stop evil once and for all. Jesus taught that he would return to judge the world. His parable of the sheep and the goats (Matthew 25:31–46) teaches a number of things about the last judgment:

- the judge will be the Messiah, who will then be King

- people will be separated into two groups

- the judgment is based on how people have acted. Those who have acted in a loving way will be rewarded. Those who have acted out of self-interest will be punished.

It is wrong to try to interpret the details of parables. They are stories which make a point. The Bible has more to say about how a person can be accepted by God (Matthew 10:22; Mark 16:16; Luke 23:39–43; John 12:44ff). The key issue is how people have responded to the person of Jesus: belief or rejection.

'Then he will say to those on his left, "Away to the eternal fire ... I was hungry but you would not feed me, thirsty but you would not give me a drink" ' (Matthew 25:41–42).

Going Through Hell...

Have you ever been lost? It's frightening to be lost in a strange place, perhaps on a mountain, cut off from those you love. People can feel that same deep sense of 'lostness' when things go badly wrong in their lives. Sometimes people say things like: 'I'm going through hell at the moment.' 'I believe in hell—I'm living through it.'

What do you think they mean when they say things like this? What could be happening in their lives to make them feel like this?

> **Write a thought bubble to say what this person might be thinking and feeling.**

Reporting live the blitz that started the Gulf War an American TV reporter said, 'Clearly I've never been there, but this feels like the centre of Hell.'

God missing

Multiply this feeling of being lost and separated from those you love a million times, and you have some idea of what Christians mean when they talk of the existence of hell.

Christians believe that hell is not simply a punishment: it is something people choose for themselves, day by day. People choose to be separated from God, just as they can choose to love God.

66 What is hell? It is the self-chosen loneliness of the man or woman who prefers self-love to the love of God. 99

MICHAEL RAMSEY

Edvard Munch (1863–1944) painted 'The Scream' to express the hell inside him. He described his childhood in the following words: 'Illness, madness and death were the black angels that kept watch over my cradle.' In 1908 he suffered what he called 'a complete mental collapse'.

What do you think?

The Bible describes hell in a very pictorial way: 'Whoever did not have his name written in the book of the living was thrown into the lake of fire' (Revelation 20:15).

Some Christians believe that the Bible should be taken literally: God cannot let evil go unpunished, or God would not be just or fair.

66 If Hitler and Stalin aren't burning or rotting in Hell, where are they? 99

BARRY HYMAN

Others find it difficult to believe in both a God of love and hell:

66 I am clear that there can be no hell for eternity. Our God could not be that cruel. However, I think for some people who have wasted every opportunity [for redemption], there may be extinction. 99

DR DAVID JENKINS

Other Christians believe in the existence of hell but do not think the picture-language of the Bible is meant to be taken literally. In the Bible people were trying to express something real and used word-pictures to describe it:

66 The Church may not require us to believe in the physical torments associated with hell, but that is not the same as saying it does not exist. 99

DAVID LUNN, BISHOP OF SHEFFIELD

The word translated 'hell' in the Bible is *Gehenna*. This referred to the Valley of Hinnom outside Jerusalem, where the city's rubbish was burned. Hell stands for the state of being cut off from God, of being thrown away. Fire can be used to destroy things but also to remake things.

Summary

Christians believe that people can choose to be separated from God for ever. They call the consequence 'hell'.

The image of a 'black hole' (below) suits the idea of hell.

Brain Engage

1 Read the story Jesus told of the rich man and Lazarus in Luke 16:19–31. How is hell pictured here? What message was Jesus trying to get across?

2 Look at E. Munch's 'The Scream'. Now draw your own symbol of hell. Give it a caption.

3 Look at 'The Scream' again. If this picture could speak what would it say?

4 If you held the key to heaven what sort of people would you let in?

That's Paradise

Where would you go for an ideal holiday—somewhere sunny with a lovely beach? Or are you the adventurous type? Write your own travel brochure called 'My idea of Paradise'.

You should cover the following:

- a description of the place (maybe a drawing)

- the accommodation

- the food

- the nightlife

- what you need to take with you

- how you get there—do you need a passport or permission to enter?

- the other people there—is anyone allowed or just the chosen few?

Departure times

Not published in advance. People must be ready to leave at a moment's notice (Acts 1:7).

Cost of tickets

Tickets must be obtained in advance. They can't be bought. They are given free to all who believe in Jesus and follow his example in the way they live (John 5:24; Romans 1:17).

Luggage allowance

Nil (1 Timothy 6:7).

Vaccinations

None needed. Heaven is disease- and pain-free (Revelation 21:4).

Accommodation

First class—already arranged (John 14:2).

Main attraction

God will be there: happiness guaranteed (Revelation 21:3).

We have already seen that Christians believe they are going somewhere. They call their destination 'heaven'; it's where God is. If hell is being lost, heaven is being found. But what do we know about it? The Bible doesn't tell us everything, but enough for a brochure! Check it out yourself.

Coming to the party?

Jesus pictured heaven as a party; a banquet which people will share with God (Luke 14:15–24).

The other side of the grave

Christians don't believe that heaven is a place in the sky. They are therefore not surprised when astronauts fail to find God in space. 'Up there' language is picture-language. Saying that God is 'above us' means that he is far greater than people can imagine.

Christians believe that their future is to enjoy a new life with God—one in which wrong and pain and death no longer figure. It involves a transformation, something like what happens to a caterpillar. A caterpillar's life is very limited; it is slow and its only interest is in eating. One day it stops eating. It spins itself into a cocoon, and turns into a chrysalis. It looks dead; its old tired life is finished. Then a miracle. Out of the chrysalis a butterfly emerges into a new free life. Unlike the caterpillar it can fly, and it is beautiful.

Christians believe that they will be raised to a new life at the end of time. Paul describes what will happen:

> 66 Our earthly bodies which die and decay are different from the bodies we shall have when we come back to life again, for they will never die. I am telling you this strange and wonderful secret: we shall not all die, but we shall all be given new bodies! It will all happen in a moment, in the twinkling of an eye . . . our earthly bodies . . . must be transformed into heavenly bodies which will live forever. 99
>
> 1 CORINTHIANS 15:42, 51–53 (LIVING BIBLE)

Helen's husband died when he was forty from a heart attack. She describes what she felt when she went to his funeral:

> 66 I couldn't believe it was happening. Only a few days ago he was so well. I felt that the world had come to a stop—I couldn't understand how everyone else could carry on with their lives as though nothing had happened.
>
> "Odd words in the service hit a chord in me: 'I am sure that neither death nor life will be able to separate us from the love of God . . .', 'We believe that Jesus died and rose again; and so it will be for those who died as Christians . . .' At that point I realized that although I had to say goodbye to Paul, God was at the same time welcoming him home. All that was precious and unique in Paul had not died—his love, his generosity and humour—all these things still lived on. 99

Brain Engage

1 How did belief in a life with God after death affect Helen?

2 Try writing a postcard from a new spiritual body to an old earthly one. What is life like? Use the Bible passages to help you.

3 Do you think belief in heaven will affect how somebody lives? Explain your answer.

Summary

Christians 'believe in . . . the resurrection of the body and the life everlasting' (Apostles' Creed).

I Believe

Credo is a Latin word which means 'I believe'. From *credo* comes the word 'creed'. A creed is a statement of what people believe.

What do you believe?

Write your own creed in which you make statements of what you believe. The lines of your creed could start with the words, 'I believe in/that...' or 'I think it is important to...'

In the early days of the church there were many arguments about what, exactly, Christians believed. So the leaders got together to agree on a statement of key beliefs. Two of the creeds they wrote—a short one called the Apostles' Creed and a longer one called the Nicene Creed—are used in church services today. They still sum up the beliefs that unite Christians in all branches of the church.

I believe that charity begins at home

I believe that when I die that's it!

I believe in a force behind the universe

The Apostles' Creed

I believe in God, the Father almighty,
    creator of heaven and earth.

I believe in Jesus Christ, his only Son, our Lord.
He was conceived by the power of the Holy Spirit
and born of the Virgin Mary.
He suffered under Pontius Pilate,
was crucified, died, and was buried.
He descended to the dead.
On the third day he rose again.
He ascended into heaven,
and is seated at the right hand of the Father.
He will come again to judge the living
    and the dead.

I believe in the Holy Spirit,
the holy catholic Church,
the communion of saints,
the forgiveness of sins,
the resurrection of the body,
and the life everlasting. Amen.

Angelina explains why Christianity is important to her.

66 The most important thing is the feeling that God is always in the background of my life. When he sent his Son into the world he was known as Emmanuel, which means God is with us. Whatever happens in life I know God is there beside me. So many people today feel as though there is no meaning to life. Although life is not always easy I know that God created me for a purpose, he values me. Even death is not to be feared because I know that I will be with him. 99

Brain Engage

1 Use Angelina's quote to make a creed—a statement of what she believes.

2 Carefully read the Apostles' Creed. Make two lists: one of all the facts it contains, and the second of all the beliefs.

3 Look carefully at what the creed tells you about Jesus. What elements of his life do they mention? Which do they miss out? What conclusions can you draw from your observations?

4 Read 1 Corinthians 15:3–8. This is Paul's statement of belief about Jesus. Turn these verses into a creed.

5 The Stamp Test
Take a piece of paper the size of a stamp. Try writing a motto or phrase to sum up the Christian message which would fit on the back of the stamp.

Summary

The Apostles' Creed is a statement of what Christians have always believed and still believe today.

Creeds for Today's World

Christianity today is a worldwide religion. People in different parts of the world have written creeds of their own to highlight important things about the Christian faith in their own circumstances. One of the creeds on this page comes from Latin America and the other from southern Africa.

Jesus was a Jew. The Jewish people had suffered under many foreign powers. At the time Jesus was born they were waiting for God to send a great leader to save them from foreign rulers. They called this 'chosen one' the Messiah. In Africa and South America, where people have for centuries been oppressed and enslaved by white Europeans, Christians stress that Jesus has come for all people, to free them from unjust suffering.

A Latin American Creed

Christians living in Latin America have stressed the fact that Jesus came to free people from slavery and exploitation. One theologian has rewritten the gospel putting it in a South American context. In it Jesus says: 'God has said: "Love your neighbour as yourself" but you oppress the weak. I demand that you stop exploiting people.'

Their creed highlights Jesus as a freedom fighter for justice and peace:

Brain Engage

1 What kind of a world is this creed describing?

2 What hopes for the future does it present?

3 What is the Christian message in this creed?

4 What do you think of a Jesus who preaches love but is pictured as a guerrilla fighter?

I believe in God, creator of an unfinished world,
I believe in God, who has not divided people into poor and rich, specialists and ignorant, owners and slaves.

I believe in Jesus Christ, who saw the world situation and who took a stand in it.
Each day I fear that he may have died in vain
because we do not live as he lived,
because we betray his message.
I believe in Jesus Christ, who rises for us
so that we may be freed from our prejudices, fear and hate,
so that we may change the world into the kingdom of God.

I believe in the Spirit, who came with Jesus into the world.

I believe in the community of all peoples,
And in our responsibility for making our world either a place of misery, hunger and violence
—or the City of God.
I believe that it is possible to build a just peace.

I believe that a life full of meaning is possible for all; and in the future of this world of God. Amen.

An African Creed from Zimbabwe

Black people have suffered for many years at the hands of white oppressors. African Christians have therefore pictured Jesus as a black Messiah. They do not mean that Jesus' skin was black. What they mean by this image is that God sent Jesus as the Messiah, or liberator, to free all people from oppression.

This 'People's Creed' reflects the belief that God works to heal the divisions between races:

I believe in a colour-blind God,
Maker of technicolour people,
Who created the universe
And provided abundant resources
    to be shared equally among all his people.

I believe in Jesus Christ,
Born of a common woman,
Who was ridiculed, disfigured, and executed,
Who on the third day rose and fought back;
He storms the highest councils of men,
    where he overturns the iron rule of
    injustice.
From henceforth he shall continue
    to judge the hatred and arrogance of
    men.

I believe in the Spirit of Reconciliation;
The united body of the dispossessed;
The communion of the suffering
    masses;
The power that overcomes the
    dehumanizing forces of men;
The resurrection of personhood,
    justice, and equality;
And in the final triumph of
    Brotherhood.

CANAAN BANANA

Brain Engage

5 From the news decide three issues you would want to include if you were writing a creed for today.

6 Take each verse of the 'People's Creed' and illustrate it. You could use pictures from magazines and newspapers to show the situation being described. Write a statement under each picture summing up the verse.
If you had to put a photo of Jesus next to this modern-day creed how would he look? How would he be dressed? What would he be doing?

Summary

The creeds written by Christians today show how their Christian beliefs affect the way they act.

Living in Harmony in Our 'Global Village'

Today, because of television, people are aware of things happening all over the world. In the modern world we have to learn to get on not only with people we live close to but with people we have never met. Our neighbours are not only those people who live down the street but also people in other countries. We depend on people all over the world for basic things like food and clothes. The big world has become a 'global village'.

Make a menu of all the food you eat in an average day. Which countries does that food come from?

How would you answer the question, 'who is my neighbour?'

Although there are about two thousand million Christians in the world today Christianity is only one of the world's major religions. Believers of all religions live alongside each other. So what do Christians believe about other religions? Christians hold a number of views:

66 Jesus said, "I am the way, the truth and the life; no one goes to the Father except by me" (John 14:6). I believe there is only one way to God. All other religions are false. 99

66 There is only one God but religions talk about God in different ways. We must respect all religions in their attempt to talk about God. 99

66 We can learn from people of different religions. By doing this we can deepen our own faith. 99

Religions have a lot in common: for example, the 'Golden Rule' about how people should treat each other:

Buddhism
66 I will act towards others exactly as I would act towards myself. 99
FROM UDANA-VARQA

Christianity
66 Do for others just what you want them to do for you. 99
JESUS, FROM LUKE'S GOSPEL

Islam
66 None of you "truly" believe, until he wishes for his brothers what he wishes for himself. 99
A SAYING OF THE PROPHET MUHAMMAD

Judaism
66 What is harmful to yourself do not to your fellow men. 99
RABBI HILLEL, FROM THE *TALMUD*

Getting on . . .

We all have to get on with people. Schools, for example, have written codes of conduct setting out how people should act if they are to get on together.

Code of Conduct at Peers School

Students at Peers have the right to an education which offers them the best opportunity to attain their potential.

Guiding Principles

In order to make this happen, it is essential that every one of us is:

- **Considerate:** respecting everyone else as an individual; making sure our words and actions do not cause offense to anybody.

- **Courteous:** being polite and helpful at all times.

- **Co-operative:** being willing to work together.

- **Friendly:** being on good terms with each other.

- **Honest:** being truthful.

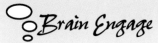

Brain Engage

1 What are the advantages of having a code of conduct?

2 How would people act without a code of conduct?

3 Is it arrogant to believe your religion is nearer the truth than someone else's? Debate this.

The World Council of Churches has written its own Code of Conduct. It sets out how people of different religious beliefs should relate to each other.

Living with people of different faiths and beliefs

Code of Conduct

- **As members of the human family, we should show each other respect and courtesy.**

    This means:

- respecting other people's freedom to express their beliefs

- trying to understand what others actually believe and value

- respecting the convictions of others about food, dress and so on, and not behaving in ways which cause offence.

- **When we talk about matters of faith with one another, we need to do so with openness, honesty and straightforwardness.**

    This means:

- recognizing that a true conversation is a two-way process

- being honest about our beliefs

- not misrepresenting other people's beliefs and practices.

- **All of us want others to understand and respect our views. In a multi-faith society, those who also want to try to convince others of the claims of their own religion need to do so with self-restraint and a concern for the other's freedom and dignity.**

    This means:

- respecting the right of others to disagree with us

- avoiding violence of action or language

- being sensitive and courteous.

Summary

We live in a global village in which people need to learn to respect each others' beliefs.

Glossary

Advent = 'coming'
The period Christians observe as preparation for Christmas.

Anglican
A Christian who is a member of the Church of England or one of the churches connected with it (such as the Church in Wales and the Church of Australia).

Apostle
One of the twelve disciples Jesus chose.

Ascension
The last appearance of Jesus in human form as he was taken up to heaven. Celebrated forty days after Easter (Acts 1:6–11).

Atonement
The belief that through Jesus' death humankind and God have been brought back together again—they become 'at one'.

Baptism
The ceremony for new members of the Christian family, in which they are immersed or sprinkled with water.

Bible
From a word meaning 'books'. The book which Christians regard as God's 'word'.

Bishop
Senior clergy in the Roman Catholic, Orthodox and Anglican churches.

Catholic = 'universal'
The catholic faith, that of the universal church throughout the world.

Charismatic
A modern movement within the church, emphasizing the work of the Spirit of God and the special gifts God gives to the church, such as healing or speaking with tongues (speaking in unknown languages).

Church
Christian people: all who belong to the 'body of Christ'. Also used of the building in which Christians worship.

Clergy
Ordained ministers.

Communion
Sharing of bread and wine in obedience to Jesus' command at the Last Supper.

Conversion
The 'turning round' of a person, to follow Jesus Christ.

Covenant
An agreement between two parties; promises are made on both sides. God makes unbreakable promises to his people.

Creation
The belief that the world was brought into being out of nothing by God.

Creed
A summary statement of religious (Christian) beliefs; often recited in worship.

Crucifix
A cross with a figure of the crucified Jesus on it.

Devil
The spirit of evil at enmity with God; the tempter of people.

Disciple
A follower of Jesus

Divine
Of God; holy.

Easter
A major Christian festival celebrating the resurrection of Jesus Christ from the dead.

Epiphany = 'appearance'
A festival based on the visit of the wise men, celebrating Jesus as God's gift to all people.

Eucharist = 'thanksgiving'
A service which re-enacts the Last Supper Jesus had with his disciples. Another word for Communion. The words 'Breaking of Bread' and 'Mass' are also used by different churches to describe the same service.

Evil
Wickedness; the opposite of good.

Faith
Trust in God.

Fall (the)
The biblical story which illustrates people turning away from God to follow their own desires.

Forgiveness
A love which puts hurt and revenge aside and heals broken relationships.

Gospel = 'good news'
The preaching of Jesus; also the accounts of his life by Matthew, Mark, Luke and John.

Heaven
The presence of God; the destiny of those who love God.

Hell
Permanent separation from God; the destiny of those who refuse God's love.

Holy Spirit
God; the third person of the Trinity, active in every Christian life and in the world.

Icon
A painting or mosaic of Jesus or a saint; used as an aid to worship, especially in the Orthodox Church.

Incarnation
The belief that God became a human person in Jesus.

Lent
A period of forty days' preparation for Easter; a time when Christians take stock of their lives. Its origin is in the forty days Jesus spent in the wilderness before his ministry began.

Liturgy
A term used to describe words and actions in services according to a set pattern. In the Orthodox Churches used to describe Holy Communion.

Methodism
A Protestant church founded through the work of John Wesley in the eighteenth century.

Minister
A member of the clergy, one who serves the church.

Miracle
A special act of God, a sign of his presence; normally used of occurrences which cannot be explained by the laws of nature.

Missionary
A person who spreads the Christian message. In the past this was normally used of people travelling to other countries.

Nativity
The birth of Jesus.

Ordained
Appointed as a Christian minister.

Orthodox
The Eastern Church, led by five senior bishops called patriarchs.

Parable
A story with a religious meaning, told to challenge people.

Pentecost (Whitsun)
A festival fifty days after Easter which celebrates the gift of God's Holy Spirit to the first Christians. The 'birthday' of the church.

Pilgrimage
A journey to a 'holy' place linked to some special event or person revered by Christians.

Presbyterian
A member of a church governed by elders all of equal rank; for example the national Church of Scotland.

Priest
A person in the Roman Catholic and Anglican Churches ordained by a bishop, with authority to celebrate the Holy Communion. (People called and trained to be ministers in the Protestant Free Churches are in general not ordained by bishops.)

Protestant
A term used to describe those Christian denominations born out of protest against unreformed Roman Catholic belief and practice in the sixteenth century.

Quakers
A popular name for those who belong to the Society of Friends, founded in the seventeenth century.

Repent
Turn away from sin and ask God's forgiveness.

Resurrection
The rising from the dead of Jesus Christ; also the rising from the dead at the end of time.

Roman Catholic
A major section of the church which accepts the authority of the Pope in Rome.

Rosary
A set of prayers in the Roman Catholic Church; also a string of 165 beads to help worshippers say these prayers.

Sacrament
A 'signpost' pointing to God; physical actions which point to spiritual changes in the Christian; an outward sign of a spiritual blessing (for instance baptism, eucharist).

Saint
A title used in the New Testament for all Christians, now normally kept for Christians whose outstanding commitment to God has been recognized by the church.

Scripture
An extract from, or part of, the Bible ('the Scriptures' = the Bible).

Second coming (the)
The belief that Jesus will return to earth to raise the dead and judge the world at the end of time.

Sermon
A public address on a religious theme, normally given within a service.

Transfiguration
The transformation in glory of Jesus Christ in the presence of three disciples (Mark 9:2–13).

Trinity
The belief that the one God makes himself known in three persons— Father, Son and Holy Spirit.

Vow
A promise (to God).

Worship
Paying honour and respect (to God).

Index